TANSTAAFL*

A Libertarian Perspective on Environmental Policy

*There Ain't No Such Thing As A Free Lunch

By Edwin G. Dolan

Version 40.0

Original material first published 1971 as TANSTAAFL*: *The Economic Strategy for Environmental Crisis*. New York: Holt, Rinehart and Winston

First published 2011 by Searching Finance Ltd, 8 Whitehall Road, London W7 2JE, UK

ISBN: 978-1-907720-26-0

Typeset by: Deirdré Gyenes

TANSTAAFL*
A Libertarian Perspective on Environmental Policy

*There Ain't No Such Thing As A Free Lunch

By Edwin G. Dolan

Version 40.0

About the author

Edwin G. Dolan is an economist and educator with a Ph.D. from Yale University. Early in his career, he was a member of the economics faculty at Dartmouth College, the University of Chicago, and George Mason University. From 1990 to 2001, he taught in Moscow, Russia, where he and his wife founded the American Institute of Business and Economics (AIBEc), an independent, not-for-profit MBA program. Since 2001, he has taught at several universities in Europe, including Central European University in Budapest, the University of Economics in Prague, and the Stockholm School of Economics in Riga, where he has an ongoing annual visiting appointment. During a break in his teaching career, he worked in Washington, D.C. as an economist for the Antitrust Division of the Department of Justice and as a regulatory analyst for the Interstate Commerce Commission. There, he contributed to a successful drive for deregulation of trucking and railroads, which reduced highway congestion and saved millions of gallons of fuel annually. When not lecturing abroad, he makes his home in Washington's San Juan Islands.

About Searching Finance

Searching Finance Ltd is a dynamic new voice in knowledge provision for the financial services and related professional sectors. Our mission is to provide expert, highly relevant and actionable information and analysis, written by professionals, for professionals. For more information, please visit www.searchingfinance.com

Contents

List of tables and figures

Introduction

The TANSTAAFL principle

In 1970, about the time the first Earth Day celebrations were attracting attention to issues of pollution, population, and resource depletion, I picked up a copy of Robert Heinlein's novel, *The Moon is a Harsh Mistress*.[1] The lunar colony where the novel is set faces a choice between business as usual, which would lead to economic collapse, food riots, and worse, or radical change toward economic and environmental sustainability. The slogan of the radical faction is TANSTAAFL – There Ain't No Such Thing As A Free Lunch. The relevance of the slogan to environmental issues is so strong that that I ended up using it as the title for the original version of this book, which was published the following year.

In its most basic application, the TANSTAAFL principle is a simple statement of reality: Everything of value has a cost. Calling something "free" doesn't make it free, it just makes it harder to trace how great the cost is and who bears it. TANSTAAFL is a much catchier way of expressing what economists call *opportunity cost* – the idea that whatever you chose to do has a cost that is measured in terms of the other things you could have done instead with the same time and resources.

Alternatively, the TANSTAAFL principle can be interpreted as a mandate for a policy of full-cost pricing. In a world where resources are scarce, everything has a cost. Scarce resources are used most efficiently when the price paid by the final user reflects all costs, including waste disposal, harm from pollution, and depletion of non-renewable resources.

---

[1] First published in a shorter form in *Worlds of If* magazine in 1965. My own copy is a December 1969 printing from G. P. Putnam's Sons.

Governments sometimes implement policies that hold prices below full cost, or even make something "free", but in the end these policies only make the total costs higher. As a simple example, consider the roads that, in some parts of the United States, are called "freeways". What is the difference between a "freeway" and a toll road? Neither of them is truly free; the difference lies in how the costs are paid. Toll roads are paid for by users; "freeways" are paid for by taxpayers.

The difference is fundamental. You don't drive on a toll road unless the trip is worth at least as much to you as the toll you pay. The threshold for taking a trip on the "freeway" is lower, so you use it more often, generating more wear on the road, more congestion, more pollution, and more political pressure to make the road wider. That already drives the cost up, but it's not the whole of it. There is also the cost of collecting the money to pay for the road. Collecting tolls is a very efficient operation. New technologies like transponders that identify your car without stopping and cameras to catch cheaters make it even more efficient. Collecting taxes is much less efficient – armies of accountants and bureaucrats are involved, and taxes have costly secondary effects when they distort the choices made by consumers, employers, and investors. As one of Heinlein's characters puts it, "Anything free costs twice as much in long run, or turns out worthless."

Finally, the TANSTAAFL principle can be understood as an ethical maxim: In a world where nothing is truly free, we have a moral duty to pay for what we take. Would you walk out of a restaurant without paying for your meal? Would you jump out of a taxi without paying the driver? If you backed your pickup into someone's Buick in the supermarket parking lot, would you drive off without leaving a note under their windshield wiper? If you have a duty to pay in those situations, why shouldn't you pay for the damage done by pollution from your car or your factory? Why shouldn't you pay the full opportunity cost of the trees you cut, the oil you pump, or the fish you catch, whether they come from someone's private property, from government property, or from an unowned commons like the oceans or the global atmosphere?

Taking the three meanings of the TANSTAAFL principle together, we can see that it is not just the moon that is a harsh mistress, but our own planet Earth is, as well. However, the fact that nothing is free does not mean that a future of sustainable prosperity is out of reach if we do things right.

First, as long as we are willing to pay for what we take, we can work together and trade with one another in ways that are truly mutually beneficial. A world of traders who follow the TANSTAAFL principle is not only more prosperous, but more environmentally friendly than one filled with bandits, fraudsters, corrupt officials, and subsidy-seeking corporate parasites, all seeking personal gain at the expense of others.

Second, a world of full-cost pricing is one that gives the maximum incentive for entrepreneurs and innovators to devise lower-cost methods of production with smaller environmental impacts, and guides consumers to choose goods and services that draw less heavily on the planet's resources.

Third, there are both economic and environmental gains to be realized from unwinding bad policies – policies that aim to produce the illusion that something is free at the expense of making it cost more in the long run. We can start making polluters pay. We can stop subsidizing wasteful housing sprawl. We can put toll booths on our "freeways." Since instituting bad policies makes things cost more, reversing them will make things cost less.

What you will find in this book

Over the years, I have often been asked to revise the original edition of this book. Every time I have looked at it, I have decided that it is unrevisable. If I started going through it line by line, it would end up being a whole new book, not a revision.

Instead, then, I have left the original text to stand on its own, and have added commentaries following each of the original chapters. The commentaries focus on the themes of what has changed and what has not changed. If you are familiar with the 1971 edition, you can read just the commentaries. If this is the first time you have seen the book, you might want to read the original chapters and the commentaries in sequence.

A few of today's major environmental issues were barely on the radar in 1971. The most prominent of them, by far, is that of climate change. My ideas on climate change are a bit too extensive to summarize in one of the chapter commentaries. Instead, I have appended an essay on the subject that was originally published in the *Cato Journal*. My thanks to the editors for their permission to reprint it.

A note on style

At the time this book was first written, standard academic writing used "he" to mean "he or she" and "man" to mean "humankind." Although those usages now sound quaint, if not offensive, I have made no stylistic changes in the original text.

Acknowledgments

I would like to thank Kitty Dolan for reading numerous drafts of the commentaries in this 40th anniversary edition and offering many suggested improvements in content and style. Bryan Caplan also read an early version; his comments helped me sharpen the argument at several points. I would also like to thank Jere Calmes, my editor on the original edition, for his repeated encouragement over the years to do a revision. Here it is, finally!

Chapter 1
WHAT ECOLOGICAL ECONOMICS IS ALL ABOUT

Searching finance

An Awareness of Threat

In the course of the sixties an increasing number of people in this country have begun to feel that despite the sustained growth of Gross National Product which we have experienced, something in the not too distant future looms as a threat to our unprecedentedly high standard of living. The word *ecology* is mentioned more and more frequently in connection with this sense of foreboding – could it be that ecology has taken over from economics as the "dismal science" of our day?

Ecology is the study of the interrelationships between organisms and their environment. It is distinct from the social sciences, which are concerned only with the interactions of creatures with other members of their own species, in that it stresses the ultimate mutual interdependence of all species of plant and animal life. Indeed, in its broadest sense ecology is simply a point of view which demands that we keep constantly in mind that *everything depends on everything else.*

This concept of universal mutual interdependence, at least within the extent of the market, has always been central to economics. The theory of general economic equilibrium teaches us that a change in the price or quantity produced of any good or service will affect the price and quantity produced of all other goods and services. A decline in the production of cattle will result in a decreased supply of leather. Up will go the price of leather, and hence of leather shoes. Consumers will buy fewer leather and more synthetic shoes. Workers will be laid off in the tanneries and taken on in plastics mills. Real estate values will fall in the neighborhood of the former and rise in the neighborhood of the latter. Eventually – according to economic science this is a literal certainty limited only by our ability to measure – the impact will be felt upon the price of eggs in China.

Ecological economics,[2] the subject of this book, accepts these concepts of general equilibrium and universal mutual

---

2 It is worth noting that etymologically the words *ecology* and *economics* are closely related. Both mean the study of, or systematization of knowledge about, the *oikos*, a Greek word meaning household.

interdependence and extends their scope to include chains of cause and effect which originate within the market, pass beyond it into the world of nature, and then return to affect human production and consumption. Sometimes the effects are direct and predictable, as when the growth of industry in the watershed of Lake Erie ruins the fishing industry there. In other cases they are dramatic and unexpected, as when the construction of the Aswan Dam in Egypt has effects which threaten to destroy more farm-land than it brings into production.

The ecological effects of economic activities which pose an increasing threat to our material welfare can be classified in many fashions. One way of looking at the problem is to draw a distinction between the cumulative environmental effects of existing production and consumption activities and the additional impact arising from future economic growth and development.

Under the heading of cumulative effects we have, in the first instance, the exhaustion of irreplaceable natural resources. When the virgin forests are cut down, the oil wells are pumped dry, and the Mesabi Range is mined out we must resort to the use of second-growth timber, oil shale, and taconite – all of which represent inferior sources which can be exploited only at increasing cost. Even these low-grade resources are not inexhaustible. Also included in the category of cumulative effects is the process of filling up irreplaceable dumping grounds with indestructible (or nearly so) waste products. For example, even if its rate of use were not to increase, the level of DDT intake of all the world's animal life would go on rising. It is already to the point where the DDT content of American mothers' milk is so high that it could not legally be bottled and sold across state lines. Likewise, the carbon dioxide content of the atmosphere, which has already risen by 14 percent so far in the 20th century, would go right on rising even if our consumption of fossil fuels were to remain indefinitely at its current level.

Yet there is no prospect whatsoever that production, population, and technology will remain static. The growth of production alone means that all the cumulative effects will accumulate at an ever-increasing rate. This would be bad enough without adding the overpopulation problem. Even in the far-from-certain event that our fields, mines, and factories can supply us with the requisite quantity of artifacts, will we be able to maintain our free and individualistic lifestyle against the sheer pressures of crowding when, by the year 2000, a world population of seven billion will have reduced elbow room per capita by more than half? Still, pollution and crowding are known horrors, and adaptable man might learn grudgingly to cope with them. It is the growth of technology which is in some ways the most frightening, since technology brings the unknown. With laboratories turning out ever more exotic drugs and chemicals at an ever-increasing rate, who will be able to test them for all their long-range and roundabout effects? How can we predict the effects of the technology of the more distant future, when we don't even know for certain what the technology of the seventies will do to us? Consider the case of the supersonic transport-scientists do not yet even know whether it will chill us by producing a layer of cirrus clouds in the stratosphere, or roast us by the greenhouse effect of the carbon dioxide it will add to the air.

Gradually, thanks to a constant stream of books, articles, speeches and TV programs, the vague ecological threat to our living standards assumes more exact contours. On one side we are faced with the prospect of simply running out of certain things which we have been consuming all along, and on the other with the prospect of devoting an ever-increasing share of our energy and ingenuity to cleaning up with our right hand the mess we make with our left.

Why are we in this quandary, and can we get out of it? The science of economics has at least some partial answers to these questions, as the next section will begin to explain.

The Spaceship Earth

Our first lesson in ecological economics will be to contrast two models – abstract, schematic representations – of human production and consumption. Kenneth Boulding has aptly called these the "throughput economy" and the "spaceship earth."

According to the throughput model, the economy is a device for withdrawing materials from exploitable "sources", processing and consuming them, and discarding the resultant waste products in pollutable "sinks". This process is diagrammed in Figure 1.1. The sources are the mines, wells, forests, and fields, while the sinks are rivers, oceans, holes in the ground, and wide-open spaces.

The spaceship earth model, in contrast, is based on the concept that the sources and sinks are one and the same, and that we, like the crew of a small spaceship on a long voyage, must reprocess and reuse everything that we consume. This model is represented schematically in Figure 1.2. In .our spaceship earth it is our natural environment, with all of its delicate ecological interdependencies, which must serve us as both source and sink for our every act of production and consumption.

We may feel complacent about the closed-loop character of our economy as long as the process by which our wastes are returned to us is sufficiently roundabout. In times of crisis, however, the feedback path may become distressingly short. Not long ago, in a small town in Kansas, a drought dried up the river upon which the town depended for its water supply. In desperation the town simply added chlorine to its own sewage effluent and pumped it back into the water mains![3]

The significance of these two models for ecological economics lies in the fact that although the spaceship earth is the more accurate representation of reality, our economic system is adapted to cope only with the throughput model.

---

[3]   This example is reported by Robert and Leona Rienow, *Moment in the Sun*, p.132

Figure 1.1 The throughput economy

Figure 1.2 The spaceship earth

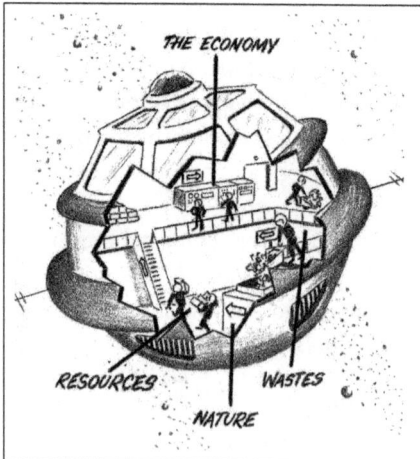

The first great defect of our throughput-oriented economic system is the way in which it distributes costs and benefits. As we have already pointed out, every action which we undertake as a producer or a consumer sets off a chain reaction which in some way affects the opportunities for production and consumption available to every other individual on the globe. In a market economy money and prices are used to keep account of the costs and benefits which this process brings to every individual. For example, you will purchase this book only if the benefit to you of reading it, as measured by the amount of money or other goods you are willing to exchange to obtain it, is sufficient to compensate the publishing house, the typesetter, the editor, the salesman, the papermaker, the inkmaker, and the author for the costs and troubles we incurred in the process of producing it. Yet, as a consumer you need to know nothing at all about the process of bookmaking to know exactly how much all of these costs will add up to, since the market price of the book summarizes them in an easily understood form.

This is what is meant when we say that the price system in a market economy is a system of social accounting which keeps track of the costs and benefits all along the chain of cause and effect set off by the production or consumption of any good.

How thorough is this accounting system? We have already seen that it keeps track of the direct costs of producing the book, but there are other types of costs which the price system in our throughput economy does a poor job of keeping account of. These are costs which result when one of those chains of cause and effect passes out of the realm of the market into the natural environment, and then sneaks back in to upset production and consumption patterns elsewhere. Does the price you pay for this book reflect the cost borne by those who live downstream from the paper mill where this page was rolled off and who have their fishing and swimming ruined? No it does not. Does the price reflect the loss to the birdwatcher who used to seek his quarry in the woodlands that were cut down to make the pulp for the paper? No. How about the neighbor to the printing plant whose sleep is disturbed by the traffic noise every night when the shift changes? Unfortunately, the price system does not keep track of this cost either.

In addition to the inability of the price system to keep accurate account of costs and benefits, our throughput economy has another serious fault. This lies in the way in which the overall results of economic activity are measured. The most popular measure of economic performance, one which we can follow closely in the newspaper, is Gross National Product. This is a figure, in the neighborhood of one trillion dollars for the United States as this book goes to press, which purports to measure the sum total value of all the goods and services produced for production and investment in the country during a year.

We are consistently taught to take pride in the GNP as a measure of our wellbeing. We doff our hats to the Japanese, whose GNP grows at a rate in excess of 10 percent per year. We shed a tear for the Nepalese, whose GNP of $50 or so per capita is the lowest in the world. And in the CIA, specialists pore over the latest data on the GNP of the Soviet Union like bookies over their racing forms. Does all this GNP fetishism make sense? Let us examine a somewhat fanciful example to see why it may not.

Suppose we have a peaceful little country with a per capita GNP of $100, all produced by the women, who work the fields in the morning and gossip in the afternoon, while the men do nothing at all but sit around and play cards and drink tea all day. Suppose now that an enterprising foreign businessman sets up a soap factory and puts all of the men to work, each producing an average of $40 worth of soap a year. Previously there was no market for soap in this pastoral nation, but now, as the soap factory is belching black coal smoke from its boilers which soil everybody's curtains, the entire output of the factory is sold to local housewives, who now spend all of their afternoons at the laundromat.

Question: What has happened to the GNP of this country? As any graduate of Economics 1 will tell you, it has gone up by 20 percent, to $120 per capita. Agricultural output has not fallen, and industrial production of $20 per capita has been introduced.

Question: What has happened to the level of wellbeing of the inhabitants of this country? They have no more to eat than before; their curtains are no cleaner than before; and they are working four times as long. Ergo, they are, let us say, about one-quarter as well-off as before.

There is a serious lesson to be learned from this little fable; namely, that GNP is not a measure of wellbeing but simply a measure of throughput. It measures the rate at which the crank is turning on that meat grinder in Figure 1.1. A person's welfare does not depend on this rate of flow of material and energy through the system, but on a state of affairs which the throughput process serves to maintain and improve. Just stop to think about it. We are happy when we can bring about a condition in which we are warm, well-clothed, stomach full, and in good company. The irksome thing about life is that just as we get this set up, it starts to go to pieces. Our house cools down; our clothes wear out; the food in our stomachs is digested and eliminated; and our friends go home when the bottle runs dry. That is where GNP comes in – it is our weapon against entropy and decay. We generate GNP in order to fuel the furnace, wash our clothes, and so forth.

Are we better off when we have more GNP? Not necessarily. Think what happens to GNP, for example, as the seasons change. In January it takes a massive rate of throughput to keep your furnace fired – lots of GNP. In the summer your air conditioner sucks up huge quantities of GNP to keep you cool. But on that rare day in spring, when you throw open all the windows and feel like a million dollars, GNP takes a nose-dive!

It would be an exaggeration to pretend that GNP and welfare are completely unrelated. When you average out things like seasonal and climatic differences there is a rough correspondence between the comfort and complexity of the state of life one tries to maintain and the amount of throughput necessary to maintain it. Clearly the fact that our per capita GNP is some thirty times that of Nepal has something to do with the fact that we are surrounded with some high multiple of the quantity of creature comforts of the Nepalese – and must keep all in working order.

Why should we quibble about GNP, which is, after all, only a number? Shouldn't we be concerned about real problems and policies instead? Unfortunately, it is impossible to separate the two, for policies are often made not on the basis of reality but on the basis of appearance. The ways in which the results of a policy are measured may crucially affect its formulation. The means our government takes to fight inflation and unemployment, erase the balance of payments deficit, or try to show a surplus in the federal budget are all crucially affected by the arbitrary choices which economists and statisticians must make among alternative ways of measuring these things.

The same is true of GNP. As long as we base our national economic goals on a number which measures throughput rather than welfare, you can be sure that the government will do everything in its power to maximize the growth of throughput regardless of the effect on welfare.

What we need is a neat, eye-catching summary statistic which will protect us from the fallacy that throughput maximization is a good thing. One simple idea, which is beginning to catch on, is simply to rename this same number and call it Gross National Cost. Another idea is to ask our statisticians to deduct from the magic number the cash value of all the damage done during the year by the spillages, leakages, seepages, emission, effluents, and cacophony that spill out of our meat-grinder economy along with the meat. Still another idea is, I think, the best of all. This is to split the current single GNP figure into two components. The first – call it Type I GNP – would measure that fraction of GNP which was produced with *renewable* resources and *recyclable* wastes. Type II GNP would then measure the total value of production which was based on the exhaustion of irreplaceable resources and the production of indestructible wastes.[4]

---

4   The idea of separating Type I and Type II GNP was suggested to me by Herbert Goertz. In a sense, it is an extreme extension of the concept of *Net* National Product, a figure derived from *Gross* National Product by deducting the sum total of depreciation of capital equipment. To arrive at Type I GNP one must also deduct the "depreciation" of all natural sources and sinks.

If this distinction were made, it would be clear that the production of clean, Type I GNP was an indisputable boon to mankind, while the output of dirty Type II GNP was at best a temporary welfare gain at the expense of further destruction of our environment. Politicians and economists would then design their policies to maximize Type I and minimize Type II. In the eyes of world opinion a high Type I component would be a source of national pride, while high production of the Type II variety would be a source of shame.

The power of statistics to determine policy should never be underestimated. If ecological economists could win the battle of the National Income Accounts their overall job would be three-quarters complete.

Ideology, Ecology, and the TANSTAAFL Principle

Faced with a steadily deteriorating environment and a set of social and economic institutions which are incapable of even correctly measuring this deterioration, let alone reversing it, an increasing number of voices are being raised with explanations of the causes of the crisis and with proposals for ending it. Although the analyses and solutions are almost as numerous and varied as the individuals propounding them, there are at least two general groupings or schools of thought – what might almost be called two ecological ideologies.

The first ideology can be called ecological evangelism. At the root of the environmental crisis the ecological evangelists see the sins of ignorance, indifference, and greed. The tone and the content of their writing is tailored accordingly.

Their tone is one of moral outrage. Very typical are the comments of Robert and Leona Rienow in the introduction to their book, *Moment in the Sun*. The authors explain how they began with thirty feet of files on the subject of the environment and the intention of writing an analytical, dispassionate study of what is happening in

America today. However, four years, twenty-five thousand miles of traveling, and countless interviews later they wrote:

> We surrendered the impossible job of impersonal analysis of a deeply personal matter. We gave up computer thinking on a subject that cannot be computerized, a subject which means your future and ours, the future of the land and the whole American people. We are involved. We are biased for beauty. We are the unblushing partisans of restraint in both exploitation and breeding. We are pluggers for a new, hard look at our misdeeds, for painful self-sacrifice, if need be, to "hold this land" and what is still on it.[5]

The content of the writing of the ecological evangelists reflects their analysis of individual moral failure as the source of the problem. They preach, first of all, of the need for ecological education and ecological enlightenment. Their first principle is that ignorance is no excuse, that it is immoral to take any action, to produce or consume any product without knowing what effects that act of production or consumption will have on the environment. If only people realized that in purchasing redwood lawn chairs and leopard skin coats they were threatening these species of plant and animal life with extinction, perhaps they would think twice before buying. And if manufacturers of new drugs, chemicals, and pesticides would simply bother to investigate the effects of their products on life cycles and food chains, instead of just marketing anything not definitely known to be harmful, perhaps much destruction could be avoided.

Next after enlightenment the evangelists preach the virtue of environmental sensitivity. They realize that ignorance is not always the problem and that, in fact, some people exist who are so insensitive to the beauty of nature that they would knowingly prefer their cheap lawn furniture to a noble stand of redwoods; would prefer a leopard lined with silk and flaunted on Fifth Avenue in New York City to one creeping through the jungles blending with light and shadow; that they would prefer the convenience of cheap newsprint

---

5   Rienow and Rienow, p. vii.

to the beauty of clear running streams and rivers; and would prefer the thrill of gunning their 400 horsepower coffin from stoplight to stoplight to having the tonic of clean air to breathe. Nonetheless, although the insensitive may be more of a problem than the ignorant, they are not beyond salvation. There is always the hope that if the beauty of nature and the banality of commercial civilization can be put into words, pictures, or testimonials sufficiently eloquent and vivid, the insensitive may be made aware of the lack of sophistication of their current tastes and be converted to the cult of nature.

After having disposed of the ignorant and indifferent, the ecological evangelists turn their energies to the last and most recalcitrant group, those avaricious and malevolent souls who would willingly and knowingly rape the wilderness to turn a profit for themselves. These, if they cannot be brought to their senses by the preaching of the Christian virtue of altruism, must then be subjected to pressure, protest, legislation, or even guerrilla action to force them into adopting a more public-spirited attitude.

At this point the ideology of ecological evangelism begins to shade over into what can be called ecological radicalism. Ecological radicals are less prone to blame the crisis on the sins of individuals and more likely to blame "the system." Very typical of ecological radicalism are the views of the editors of *Ramparts*, who recently wrote:

> ... as long as society organizes production around the incentive to convert man's energies and nature's resources into profit, no planned, equable (sic), ecologically balanced system of production can ever exist....

> We must, in short, junk the business system and its way of life, and create revolutionary new institutions to embody new goals – human and environmental.

> All this sounds utopian. Well, utopias are relative. More utopian by far than revolution is the idea that the present society, dominated by business, can create lasting, meaningful

reforms sufficient, for example, to permit mankind to survive this century.[6]

The cumulative effect of the voices of the ecological evangelists, of ecological radicals, and of ordinary concerned citizens to whom no ideological label applies is to produce increasingly irresistible demands for massive governmental action to do something now to stop the deterioration of the environment. Washington responds as best it knows how, with a plethora of proposals to ban this or that product, regulate this or that industry, require this or that device, or purchase this or that tract of land for a national park.

Speaking now as an economist, as an economist with a definite concern for piloting our spaceship earth safely through the ecological crisis with which we are increasingly undeniably faced, I must say that listening to all of this ecological dialogue sets off a great number of red flashing warning lights on my control panel. These warn that in the name of ecological salvation we are in danger of being led by men of the greatest good will and the best intentions down the road to some grave social and economic mistakes, which have been made too many times before in too many countries to bear repeating here and now again. I will mention just three of these dangers before going on, in succeeding chapters, to suggest some means for avoiding them.

The first warning light flashes when I hear the call for self-sacrifice and self-restraint as the means for resolving the environmental crisis. Any economist worth his salt knows that altruism is notoriously weak as a force for social change, and that the goal of avoiding ecological disaster will be more easily and rapidly reached by methods which harness the strong human motivations – the greed, avarice, and self-interest of individuals within the ranks of business, government, and consumers. We simply do not have time to wait for an ethical revolution before we clean up.

The second warning light flashes when I hear impassioned and contemptuous denunciations of the tastes and values of affluent

---

6   *Ramparts,* May 1970, p. 4.

American consumers. Again, impatience is part of the reason for these misgivings. Knowing how slow to change are the underlying preference systems of the individuals who inhabit our society, the economist tends to seek more speedy solutions to social problems which work within current tastes and preferences. An equal cause for concern is that certain special interest elites among environmental activists will take advantage of the genuine common interest in environmental reform, shared by all the people, to shape public policy to suit their own allegedly superior tastes and preferences.

The third warning light on my panel goes off when I hear demands that the business system, the profit motive, and private property be scrapped in favor of a "planned, equitable, and ecologically balanced system of production." Application of elementary principles of economics suggests that the path to a planned, equitable, and ecologically balanced system of production is more likely to be through a strengthening of the business system, private property, and the profit motive than through their abolition. Even if there were no other evidence, a look at the wholesale rape of the environment which has been conducted in the name of building socialism in the planned economy of the Soviet Union should be sufficient proof.[7]

But the purpose of this book is not simply to criticize the well-intentioned suggestions of others. More importantly, it is to expound a constructive strategy of its own for coping with the environmental crisis.

The fundamental principle on which this strategy is built may be expressed in a simple slogan – There Ain't No Such Thing As A Free Lunch – the "TANSTAAFL principle" for short.[8] The TANSTAAFL principle is closely related to the fundamental theorem of ecological

---

7   See Marshall Goldman, "The Convergence of Environmental Disruption," *Science*, October 2, 1970

8   The fundamental importance of this principle, and the expression itself, were impressed upon me by Robert Heinlein's fascinating ecological novel, *The Moon Is a Harsh Mistress* (New York: George Putnam's Sons, 1966). Students of the natural sciences will recognize the close relationship between the TANSTAAFL principle and the Second law of Thermodynamics.

economics, that everything depends on everything else. Everything worth while has a cost. Whenever you think you are getting something for nothing, look again – someone, somewhere, somehow is paying for it. Behind every free lunch there is a hidden cost to be accounted for.

The task of ecological economics is to figure out how to restructure the economic system so that these hidden costs will be brought out into the open, with the ultimate aim that no one who benefits from the use of the environment will be able to escape without paying in full. The rest of this book is devoted to working out specific applications of this general strategy in order to deal with specific problems.

First, Chapter 2 will review some of the basic principles of economics which lead to the conclusions suggested in this introduction. Without some basic tools of analysis there is no hope for raising the discussion of economics and ecology above the level of unsubstantiated polemic. With these tools in hand we will then examine in more detail the weaknesses of our social and economic system which have led us to the point of crisis.

Chapter 3 will demonstrate that it is possible to construct a condemnation of the polluters and abusers of our environment on a sound rational basis, without resort to the weaker support of romantic emotionalism or offended special interest. It will be shown that stopping the destruction of the environment, properly considered, is not the special interest of any group but is in an important sense in the general interest of all, polluters and victims alike. Some guidelines will be offered for public policy in the area of pollution control.

Chapter 4 will add the *caveat* that despite the demonstrable existence of a common interest in environmental improvement, there are many pitfalls in the path of any attempt to organize politically for the realization of this common interest. In addition, some further theoretical tools will be introduced as a basis for the discussion of three special problems. These are the problem of population control, in Chapter 5, the problem of economic development and the international allocation of resources, in Chapter 6, and the problem of preserving the wilderness, in Chapter 7.

The concluding chapter will turn attention from these microeconomic problems to discuss some important issues of ecological macroeconomics, such as, can man survive?

Commentary

What has changed

One thing that has changed over the years is terminology. The 1971 edition of this book used the term *ecological economics*, defined as the extension of the ideas of general equilibrium and universal interdependence to chains of cause and effect that originate within markets, pass beyond them into the world of nature, and then return to affect human production and consumption. Today, much of the subject matter of the book goes instead by the name *environmental economics*. That is how the field is described in most textbook titles and university course catalogs.

I am not sure the change is all to the good. The term environmental economics too easily leads to thinking of the economy and the environment as two separate systems, one being a realm of production and consumption, the other being a natural world that surrounds it, but remains distinct from it. That is a very different way of looking at things from the Spaceship Earth model that lies at the heart of the original Chapter 1.[9]

A crude expression of the view that the economy and the environment are separate systems is found in the popular slogan, "Drill Baby, Drill!" People who invoke that phrase seem to think that achieving a robust, growing economy is possible only if the natural

---

[9] While "environmental economics" now predominates, "ecological economics" lives on as a lesser branch of the discipline, with its own array of journals, blogs, and scholarly conferences. An early and widely cited manifesto of ecological economics, written in the 1990s by Stephen Farber and Dennis Bradley, defines the field in these terms: "*Ecological economics* recognizes that humans and their economies are parts of larger natural ecosystems and co-evolve with those natural systems. There is a material and energy basis for the relations between human economies and their ecosystems, defining not only economic, but social, structures and processes. ... Economies are inextricably embedded in larger natural ecosystems, and exchange flows of materials and energy with natural systems." ("Ecological Economics," unpublished or publisher unknown, no date (mid-1990s?), downloaded April 22, 2011 from http://www.fs.fed.us/eco/s21pre.htm.)

environment is treated as having no value in and of itself, aside from serving as a set of sources and sinks for production and consumption. In that view, the economy is measurably better off the more rapidly the sources are emptied. Similarly, when economic activities produce wastes, it is best for the economy to dispose of them in whichever sinks are closest and most convenient, those that minimize the cost of waste disposal as measured on the cash flow statements of firms and households.

True devotees of "Drill Baby, Drill!" have active contempt for butterflies, polar bears, and clean air. You're not a "real man" if you care about that wussy stuff. Orthodox environmental economists are not so open about it. They profess concern for environmental protection in principle, provided such protection can be justified by the standards of cost-benefit analysis.

Suppose, for example, the policy under discussion is how tightly to restrict sulfur dioxide emissions from coal-fired power plants. The standard approach of environmental economics begins by measuring source-costs – for example, the higher cost of lower-sulfur coal and the capital costs of scrubbing the sulfur from cheaper, high-sulfur coal. Next it measures sink costs – the damage from dumping sulfur dioxide into the atmosphere. Cost measures include things like lower crop yields, days lost from work because of respiratory disease, and higher maintenance costs for buildings and bridges. When everything is measured that can be, the job is considered to be done.

The cost-benefit approach to environmental economics

I see two problems with the reduction of environmental economics to mere cost-benefit analysis.

The first is that cost-benefit analysis short-changes subjective valuations. In the market place, subjective values are king. No real free-marketeer would criticize a consumer who pays an outrageous price for the purely subjective added value of a pair of designer shoes when, objectively speaking, a cheaper pair of no-name shoes would provide the same wear and comfort. Somehow, though, when economists put on their cost-benefit hats, they tend to down-play values that are subjective and hard to measure – things like the loss of natural beauty, extinction of species (other than those that have been commercialized), and even pain and suffering by people whose health is damaged by pollution (as opposed to measurable medical outlays). Unfortunately, revenues from production and outlays for pollution abatement are often less subjective and there-fore more easily measured than the benefits of conservation and a clean environment, which often have large subjective components.

Measuring subjective values is notoriously difficult. One mistake is simply to assume that if something cannot be measured, it is not worth taking into account when formulating policy. If that is done, cost-benefit analysis takes on a bias in favor of economic activity and against environmental protection that too easily degenerates into a version of "Drill Baby, Drill!" dressed in econometric cloth-ing. The opposite mistake is to accept too readily mere expressions of opinion or sentiment as indications of willingness to pay. Just asking people, out of context, how much should be spent to protect the polar bear or the spotted owl is not likely to produce a number that can be usefully balanced against the costs of protection.

In Chapter 7, we will see that it is sometimes possible to trans-form subjective environmental values into values objectively expressed through a willingness to pay. That is what organizations like the Nature Conservancy and Ducks Unlimited do when they mobilize voluntary contributions and spend them in the market-place to protect environmentally valuable habitat. When that cannot be done, cost benefit analysis remains a highly imperfect tool for balancing subjective benefits against objective costs.

The second problem with the cost-benefit approach to environ-mental economics is the leap that is routinely taken from analysis to policy recommendation. Let's return to the example of sulfur dioxide pollution and the acid rain it contributes to. Suppose that both objective and subjective costs and benefits are somehow accu-rately measured, and after doing so, it turns out that the harm to my pond and woodlot, which lie downwind from your power plant, are less than the cost to you of installing a stack scrubber or switching to low-sulfur coal. Are those cost-benefit calculations sufficient to support a policy of allowing you to continue unabated polluting?

I would say no – not, at any rate, if you believe in property rights, including, of course, property rights to one's own person. A regime of property rights requires that you pay for what you take. Cost-benefit analysis often rejects that principle, at least implicitly. If analysis shows that total benefits of a policy are greater than the costs, that policy is recommended for implementation, regardless of whether those on whom the costs fall are compensated by those who gain the benefits. But should a favorable balance of costs and benefits really be an excuse for uncompensated taking?[10]

Suppose you were caught shoplifting a magnum of Veuve Clicquot from your local wine merchant. Would you expect to be able to use a cost-benefit defense in court? Would you expect it to be enough to show that you valued the bottle at $75, perhaps by showing you had paid that much for similar bottles in the past, while showing that the merchant's loss was only the $50 whole-sale price paid when the wine was placed in stock? I doubt if most judges would be favorably impressed. They would say that demonstrating your willingness to pay is not enough. If you don't actually make the payment, you are a common thief, no matter how refined you palate for champagne.

Comparing the cost-benefit approach to environmental policy with the property rights approach reveals a tension between two interpretations of the TANSTAAFL principle. The interpretation of TANSTAAFL as a mandate for full-cost pricing is driven by efficiency. A policy that requires people to pay full costs provides an

---

10 The question of whether compensation should be paid for harm from pollution damage is related to, but distinct from, the question of who owns the relevant property rights to begin with. Ownership of surface rights to land comes with a package of rights to the airspace above it, the ground water below it, surface water flowing through it, wild animals that cross it, and so on. The shape of the package may vary from time to time and place to place, and those details need to be taken into account when deciding who owes compensation to whom for a given act of pollution. The point made here is that the issue of compensation cannot simply be dismissed as irrelevant once the overall balance of costs and benefits has been computed.

incentive for people not to pollute or deplete resources beyond the point where the costs of doing so exceed the benefits. That will be true regardless of the mechanism used to generate the appropriate price signal: a free-market purchase from the original owner of rights to use a source or sink, a tax per unit of pollution that accrues to a government treasury, or the purchase of a pollution permit from a third party under a cap-and-trade program.

In contrast, the interpretation of TANSTAAFL as an ethical maxim is driven by justice. That interpretation finds its institutional embodiment in the common law of property rights and related branches of the law, including torts and contracts. Common law focuses on compensation for value received and restitution for harms done. Efficiency is a by-product, a result of voluntary exchange within a framework of law, not an end in itself. If you cause harm by pollution – even the residual amount of pollution that remains after you have made the economically optimal expenditures on abatement – justice requires that you pay for resources you use and compensate victims for any personal injury or property damage that you cause. Unfortunately, that point is too often neglected in the policy prescriptions of orthodox environmental economics.

What has not changed

One thing that has not changed is that today, as in 1971, there are many who see capitalism as the source of all environmental ills and socialism as the path to sustainability. That school of thought is often called *ecosocialism*. Let's look briefly at the ideals of ecosocialism, and then at socialism and the environment in the real world.

One source for the ecosocialist critique of capitalism is the *Belem Ecosocialist Declaration*,[11] which was the product of a conference held in Paris in 2007. The declaration sets out a simple chain of cause and effect: Capitalism requires profit, profit requires growth,

---

[11] "Belem Socialist Declaration," The International Ecosocialist Network, http://www.ecosocialistnetwork.org/Docs/Mfsto2/BelemDeclaration.htm

and growth means environmental destruction. Here are some excerpts:

> Humanity today faces a stark choice: ecosocialism or barbarism. . . . We need no more proof of the barbarity of capitalism, the parasitical system that exploits humanity and nature alike. Its sole motor is the imperative toward profit and thus the need for constant growth. . . . Capitalism's need for growth exists on every level, from the individual enterprise to the system as a whole. The insatiable hunger of corporations is facilitated by imperialist expansion in search of ever greater access to natural resources . . . . The capitalist economic system cannot tolerate limits on growth; its constant need to expand will subvert any limits that might be imposed . . . because to do so would require setting limits upon accumulation – an unacceptable option for a system predicated upon the rule: Grow or Die!

Let's be right up front about it: the critique is not all wrong. The "Drill, Baby, Drill!" version of capitalism, with its throughput mentality and its contempt for environmental values, provides ample fodder for the ecosocialist critique. Still, as I wrote in 1971, the ecosocialist critique of capitalism sets off flashing red lights. To see why, we need to ask two crucial questions:

- ◆ Which has been more environmentally destructive *in practice*, capitalism or socialism?
- ◆ Which system, capitalism or socialism, is more receptive to the changes that need to be made to achieve long-run environmental sustainability?

Already in 1971, it was evident, to anyone who cared to look, that the world's preeminent experiment in socialism, the Soviet Union, had serious environmental problems. The original edition of this book cited an early paper on the topic by Marshall Goldman, "The Convergence of Environmental Destruction." Since that time we have learned much more about environmental destruction under Soviet socialism. Throughout the Soviet period, Goldman continued to research the topic in books such as *The Spoils of*

Progress.[12] In the 1980s, Mikhail Gorbachev's policy of *glasnost*, followed in the 1990s by the collapse of the Soviet Union, made access to Soviet environmental information easier for later authors such as Murray Feshbach and Alfred Friendly, Jr., who provided a thorough survey in *Ecocide in the USSR.*[13]

The environmental sins of Soviet Socialism were many and are much better known now than they were four decades ago. The books just cited, and many other sources as well, discuss these and other examples in detail:

- ◆ Pollution of Lake Baikal, the world's oldest, deepest, and once cleanest body of fresh water, caused by paper mills and other industries that dumped untreated waste into the lake.

- ◆ The near-disappearance of the once-vast Aral Sea, which dried up due to diversion of water for irrigation, leaving behind salt deserts poisoned by agricultural chemicals.

- ◆ The Chernobyl nuclear disaster, the world's worst, caused not just by operating errors but by a reckless design that provided no containment vessel in case of accident. (The nuclear accident that had been considered the world's worst before Chernobyl also occurred in the Soviet Union, namely, the 1957 explosion of a waste storage pond at the Mayak nuclear weapons complex.)

- ◆ Disastrous peat fires in the Moscow region, a legacy of ill-conceived Soviet projects for draining the local wetlands.

- ◆ Enormous emissions of greenhouse gasses, due to heavy reliance on coal and far lower energy efficiency than capitalist economies.

- ◆ High levels of air pollution in major cities, caused by factories sited close to populated areas and operating with minimal if any pollution controls.

- ◆ Destructive farm and forestry practices, leading to widespread erosion and habitat loss.

---

12 Marshall Goldman, *The Spoils of Progress*, MIT Press, 1972.
13 Murray Fishback and Alfred Friendly, Jr., *Ecocide in the USSR*, Basic Books, 1992.

China, the world's other big socialist economy, also has its long list of environmental sins. Due in large part to intensive use of coal, it has recently taken the world lead in greenhouse gas emissions, despite an economy smaller in absolute size than that of the United States. In air quality, it is home to 16 of the world's 20 most polluted cities. Water pollution is a pervasive disaster. China's leadership in production of rare earth metals was achieved largely due to illegal pirate mining that caused intense heavy metal pollution and local health calamities. An increasing percentage of pollutants, from mercury to soot, that are deposited in the western United States are being traced all the way to China.

To their credit, ecosocialist documents like the *Belem Declaration* direct at least token criticism at what they call "productivist socialism" as practiced in the Soviet Union and China. I think the ecosocialists are on to something, when they introduce this concept, although not perhaps quite what they think.

The adjective *productivist,* as applied to an economy, appears to mean one that concentrates on maximizing output without paying sufficient attention to the costs of inputs. By "costs of inputs," of course, I mean what economists call *opportunity costs,* that is, costs measured in terms of the value of alternative uses for the same resources. Opportunity costs of industrial production include both the costs of depleting non-renewable resources (lost opportunities to use the same resources for some other purpose in the future) and external costs (for example, the lost opportunities to use or enjoy property damaged by pollution).

If we understand the term in this way, then there is not only such a thing as productivist socialism, but also a productivist capitalism. The "affordable energy" lobby in the United States is an example of productivist capitalism in action. Affordable energy is a favorite slogan of the American Petroleum Institute, as used, for example, by API President Jack Gerard, who comments that regulation of offshore drilling will hurt growth "by undercutting our nation's access to affordable, reliable, domestic sources of oil and natural gas."[14]

What the affordable energy lobby is worried about are attempts to raise the price of gasoline at the pump by enough to cover external costs of petroleum production and use. In the case at hand, Gerard was worried about regulations aimed at ensuring that oil companies bear the cost of oil spills and of precautions needed to avoid them. At other times, the same affordable energy argument has been directed at regulations intended to control air pollution, both on a local level and in the form of global climate change.

It is a fact that businesses seek profit, going after any and all profit opportunities. We cheer when entrepreneurs increase profits by improving products or reducing production costs. However, profits can also be boosted by lobbying the government to restrict the activities of competitors, and, equally, by lobbying for laws that allow companies to shift part of their costs of production to unwilling third parties. OK, so you don't want to call those profits? I agree. Economists call them "rents," but that term is too wonky for many people. Ayn Rand had a better term: *Loot*. Polluters are looters.

The critique of productivism

Let's come back now to the ecosocialist critique of capitalism. What it really comes down to is a critique of productivism. The question we have to ask is, which system, capitalism or socialism, is more susceptible to productivist tendencies? I think the answer is socialism, although capitalism is by no means immune.

The first reason that socialism is more likely to develop environmentally harmful productivist tendencies is that economic incentives do not work very well under socialism. In a capitalist society, the single most useful tool of environmental policy is to ensure that market prices fully recognize all externalities. If the price of gasoline at the pump fully reflects the opportunity costs

---

14 Comment made to CNN at the height of the BP oil spill, May 29, 2010, downloaded from http://money.cnn.com/2010/05/28/news/companies/ BP_safety_review/?postversion=2010052921.

of pollution and resource depletion, drivers, regardless of their personal environmental sensitivities, will be forced to think about driving less or buying more efficient vehicles. The same applies to users of industrial inputs, whether they be plastics makers, farmers, or power plants.

I don't mean to underestimate the difficulty of getting the legislature of a democratic capitalist country to pass the laws needed to ensure that market prices reflect environmental values. Still, when the price system is used to fight pollution, it seems to work. For example, in the United States of the 1990s and early 2000s, a system of tradable permits was used with great success to bring down sulfur dioxide emissions from coal-burning power plants, with the result that the intensity of acid rain in the eastern part of the country was cut by half.

Under socialism, economic incentives to fight pollution do not work as well. Yes, I know, there is such a theoretical construct as "market socialism." Under that hypothetical system, advocated by 20th century writers such as Oskar Lange and Abba Lerner, managers of collectively owned firms guide their production activities in accordance not with true market prices set by supply and demand, but instead "shadow prices" set by government planners at levels supposedly equal to opportunity costs. In theory, there would be no reason why the shadow prices could not include appropriate adjustments for environmental values. I don't want to re-argue the whole market socialism debate here. The concept has been widely judged to be impractical, and as far as I know, it has no living proponents. I think Ludwig von Mises said it all when he suggested that a real market is to market socialism as a real railroad is to a boy playing with toy trains. So instead, let's look at real world socialism.

In the Soviet variant of socialism, the problem was not so much that industrial managers were insensitive to environmental cost incentives as that they were insensitive to any kind of cost incentive at all. The Soviet system did not just encourage environmental waste, it was wasteful in every conceivable way. It wasted labor, capital, energy, natural resources, cement, steel, coal, tractors, fertilizer, wood, water – it wasted everything. Why? Because there was no profit motive.

Today, some people worry that big banks like Goldman Sachs do not operate efficiently because they know the government will bail them out if they make a loss. This is called "privatizing the gains, socializing the losses." Well, the Soviet economy was a system in which *every* enterprise was a Goldman Sachs. No wonder it collapsed.

Now for the second reason why socialism tends to be more productivist than capitalism. This one has to do with social attitudes that arise when there are no property rights. Where there are property rights, there is always an owner to resist trespass, whether by people on foot or by noxious chemicals wafting through the air. True, the legal system doesn't work perfectly. Sometimes owners can't adequately protect their rights, but the rights are there. Also, where there is widespread ownership of at least small scraps of property, respect for the property rights of others becomes widespread as well, although, alas, not universal.

But wait, the ecosocialist might say, under socialism there are collective property rights and respect for the property of society as a whole. Really? Let me tell a story.

At the business school my wife and I used to run in Moscow, the students put on an annual May picnic. After some advance scouting by the class president, the entire student body and faculty would jump on the electric commuter train. A few stops outside the city, we would jump off and head into the woods for a nice picnic. Whose woods? Some ministry's or institute's or collective farm's; no one ever seemed to know exactly.

A picnic needed a campfire, of course, so someone would bring an ax and cut down the nearest sapling to make a fire. When cleanup time came, the students followed their standard practice, which was to toss all the beer cans and vodka bottles into the remnants of the campfire, where they would become broken, charred, and harder to pick up in the unlikely event that someone were to try to do so later. When we suggested bringing our own firewood or packing out our garbage, we were met by looks that suggested such things had never been thought of before.

I started asking friends and colleagues about all this. Why didn't the socialist property owner care who picnicked there? Why didn't kids learn to respect socialist property, and clean up after themselves? The answer was that people didn't think of those woods as socialist property, even though nominally, they were. Instead, they were seen as *nich'ia sobstvennost* – "no one's property". As such, no one took responsibility for them, and no one felt bad about abusing them. Extend the same attitude to Lake Baikal, the Aral Sea, and the Chernobyl nuclear station, and what you get is Soviet socialism.

The third reason that socialism tends to be more productivist than capitalism stems from political economy. Private property gives political power bases to multiple interests. Sometimes that can work against the environment, as when Appalachian coal unions and mine owners join to lobby against restrictions on sulfur dioxide emissions. At the same time, though, producers of low-sulfur coal from Western states can lobby on the other side, achieving some kind of balance. Furthermore, not-for-profit groups can use the mechanisms of private property to protect critical habitat, and private ownership sustains an independent voice for media that can publicize environmental causes. Even ecosocialists enjoy the protection of private property for their web sites and conferences.

In a socialist system, producers have a stronger grip on the levers of political power. After all, as state enterprises, they are not mere lobbyists – they are themselves a part of the government structure. For example, Marshall Goldman notes that there were protests in the Soviet Union when paper mills first started dumping waste into Lake Baikal. However, the protesters themselves were always one government institution, say, the Limnological Institute of the Academy of Sciences, working against another, in this case the Ministry of Timber, Paper, and Woodworking. Sometimes the protesters were able to exploit personal rivalries within the government in order to plant articles in government newspapers, but in the end, they always lost. The whole incentive system of the Soviet economy, from the Politburo down to the local plant manager, was focused on just one thing: meeting the impossibly demanding production targets of the Five Year Plans. The environment always lost.

Once again, let me emphasize that private property and a market economy may be necessary conditions for protection of the environment, but they are not sufficient conditions. The sad story of environmental protection in post-Soviet Russia is a case in point. Socialism no longer reigns in Russia, but the variant of capitalism that has replaced it is no less productivist. Civil society is weak. Green protesters still struggle to get publicity for their causes in a largely state-controlled press. It is no longer casual picnickers who chop down the saplings in Moscow's green belt, but instead, billionaire oligarchs who fence off whole swathes of protected habitat for their sprawling dachas. Oil is king, and a blind eye is turned to spills on land or at sea. BP, chased from the Gulf of Mexico with its tail between its legs, is getting ready to drill for oil among the drifting icebergs off Russia's northern coast. The last wild Siberian tiger may soon fall to a shot from the helicopter of an oligarch or government minister out for a weekend's "sport".

Are things better in China, where private industry has made huge inroads into the still nominally socialist economy? Now and then there are a few hopeful signs. This year has seen a belated campaign to shut down some of the worst pirate rare-earth mines in favor of more cleanly operated government ventures. China has become a leader in alternative energy, although its efforts may reflect an opportunistic effort to corner the world market for windmills and solar panels rather than a genuine concern for the planet. Meanwhile, urban air pollution remains so bad that the Olympics could be staged in Beijing only by shutting down most local industry for the duration. I sit here in my house in Washington State wondering how much Chinese mercury is coming down from the rain clouds that drift in across the Pacific. But at least I won't have to get the approval of a socialist censor to rant about it in my blog.

Chapter 2

PRINCIPLES OF ECONOMICS IN ONE EASY LESSON

Searching
finance

Picture two men who are having a race. Each is given certain equipment at the starting line: 1. a pair of tennis shoes, and 2. a box of bicycle parts. When the starting gun goes off each man can proceed in either of two ways. He can put on the tennis shoes and start running toward the finish line or, alternatively, he can sit down, assemble the bicycle, and then ride it to the finish. Which is the best way to win the race? Clearly, the answer depends on the length of the racecourse. If it were one hundred yards, there is no doubt that it would be faster to run. But if it were twenty-five miles or more, the bicycle method would probably be the best bet-the rider would breeze past the exhausted runner at about the fifteen-mile mark and coast on to an easy victory.

Economists deal with situations like this every day. The time you put in on the starting line getting your equipment ready is called *investment* – a term denoting activity that does not in itself get you any closer to your goal but which allows you to proceed faster later on. The optimal amount of investment depends, among other things, on how big a job you have to do.

Getting through this little book on ecological economics is a medium-sized job, so before proceeding, we will digress to make a medium-sized investment in some special concepts and terminology. Any reader who thinks he can run faster than he can ride can skip ahead to the next chapter, but it isn't advisable.

Marginalism and the Law of Supply and Demand

The first useful economic concept needed in succeeding chapters is that of *marginalism*. Economists are always talking about marginal this and marginal that because most of the important economic decisions made in this world are marginal decisions – whether to do a little bit more of this or a little bit more of something else – rather than large, all-or-nothing decisions. For example, we notice that although an occasional consumer may come to a spiritual crisis in his life and, as a matter of religious principle, decide to foreswear meat and become a vegetarian, most consumers do not make all-

or-nothing decisions concerning meat and vegetables. Instead, they make marginal decisions such as whether to buy ten carrots and five slices of salami, or to cut back by one carrot in order to get one more slice of salami. In business, marginal decisions are also the focus of everyday attention. Although occasionally momentous, all-or-nothing decisions may be made, such as whether or not to build a transcontinental railroad (there is, by definition, no such thing as half a transcontinental railroad) most railroad managers spend most of their time making thousands of small decisions – whether to add one more car to the 2:52 train from Chicago to Minneapolis. Even economic changes which in retrospect appear to be radical and sweeping (the Industrial Revolution, the mechanization of agriculture) usually turn out, upon close inspection, to have been composed of a great many small, marginal decisions.

Economists who have analyzed the behavior of individuals and households in their role as consumers have found that consumer decisions made according to the marginal principle best serve the goal of gaining maximum benefit from a limited budget. In deciding whether or not to make a marginal increase in his consumption of one item the consumer must judge whether the *marginal benefit* of extending consumption in this direction is sufficient to compensate for the loss of the opportunity to extend his consumption in some other direction. For example, at the lunch counter if I spend a dime on one more cup of coffee, I must forego the opportunity to spend that dime on one more donut; hence, before I make the decision I subconsciously ask myself whether the marginal benefit I would receive from a dime's worth of coffee is greater than that from a dime's worth of donut.

It seems to be an almost universal law of consumer behavior that as a person consumes more and more of a given good, the marginal benefit to him of still more of it becomes less and less. That first piece of chocolate cake may be delightful; the second is merely good; the third is about all that the consumer can hold; and the fourth may send him off to the vomitorium. This is the law of *diminishing marginal benefit*.

The law of diminishing marginal benefit is what guarantees that the normal consumer will purchase a wide variety of goods, for if he bought too much of a single item its marginal benefit would fall below that of the foregone opportunities, and he would not be getting the most benefit for his money. This is just common sense. The only time the law of diminishing marginal benefit seems to be violated is in the phenomenon of addiction. The addict, craving more of the object of his habit the more he consumes, may spend every cent he has on this one thing.

In the business world the marginal concept is also central to the decision-making process, but this time it is *marginal cost* which is the focus of attention. The typical avaricious Capitalist, always looking for a way to increase his profits, will produce anything which he thinks he can sell above the cost. Suppose, for example, he owns a farm and is trying to decide whether or not to plant a few more turnips. If an additional pound of turnips can be sold for ten cents, he will simply compare this to the marginal cost of growing a pound of turnips. If the marginal cost of turnips is, say, five cents a pound, he will be able to pocket a five-cent profit after paying his costs out of the increased sales revenue.

What keeps greedy Capitalists from turning the whole world into one giant turnip patch? Two things. First of all, there is the law of diminishing returns, which says that if you devote more and more resources to any given line of production, eventually the marginal cost of production will rise. In the case of turnips, eventually you will run out of good turnip fields and have to grow your turnips in poorer fields where each additional pound of turnips will cost you eight, ten, even twenty cents. And when the marginal cost goes above the price any smart Capitalist will get out of the turnip business, since the opportunity for profit will be gone.

Second, the law of diminishing marginal benefit puts another brake on the expansion of turnip production. Although consumers may at first eagerly snap them up at ten cents, as the market is flooded with an ever-greater supply of turnips, the benefit of an additional turnip, and hence the price which a customer will pay for it, will gradually fall. The falling marginal benefit will at some point meet the rising marginal cost and a price will be established, perhaps eight cents a pound, where there will be no further incentive to expand production.

Taken together, the law of diminishing marginal benefit and the law of diminishing returns (that is, increasing marginal costs) form the basis for the famous *law of supply and demand*. The amount of a good *demanded* by consumers depends on its price because, desiring to get the most for their money, they will purchase it only as long as its marginal benefit exceeds its price. With diminishing marginal benefits, this means a .fall in the price will induce consumers to buy more, and a rise in the price to buy less. The amount of a product *supplied* by producers also depends on price – but because of increasing marginal costs, suppliers will step up their output only if the price rises, and will cut back when it falls. If, at a given price, the desired purchases of consumers exceed the desired sales of producers, the pressure of unsatisfied customers competing to buy a limited supply will bid up the price, and will, consequently, call for a greater supply of the good. If the price is such that desired sales exceed desired purchases, the opposite happens; unsatisfied sellers, competing for a limited number of customers, drive the price down, inducing the customers to buy more.

Somewhere between these two possibilities is a point where the desired sales of suppliers and desired purchases of consumers just match. The forces of the market always tend to drive the price toward this point, which is the point where marginal benefit = price = marginal cost.

Efficiency and the Equimarginal Principle

Marginalism is just one of the peculiar concepts that economists always seem to be hung up about. Another of equal importance is the concept of *efficiency*. The common dictionary definition of efficiency is the quality or property of acting or producing with a minimum of waste, expense, or unnecessary effort. That's actually not a bad definition, and if we were to limit ourselves to it, we could probably get along fairly well. Still, as long as this is a book on economics we may as well use the more pedantic sounding but more interesting technical definition favored by economists. An economy is said to be efficient at a given moment in time if, and only if, there is no way in which goods and services can be redistributed among consumers, or production tasks reassigned among producers, in such a way that as a result the welfare of at least one individual is increased without a decrease in the welfare of any other individual.

The economic definition of efficiency allows us to deal with certain situations where the ordinary definition would seem awkward. For example, what about the possibility mentioned above that the entire world might be turned into a gigantic turnip plantation? Suppose that all the men, land, and machines in the world were put to work producing turnips, all using the most modern techniques and working with an absolute minimum of waste, expense, or unnecessary effort. Would this be an efficient use of the world's resources? According to the dictionary' definition, yes. According to the economic definition, no.

The turnip plantation model of the world economy would not be efficient because it ignores the law of diminishing marginal benefits, and its corollary that in diversity is bliss. (We will not consider the possibilty that all the world's consumers are turnip addicts.) A man-hour diverted from turnip production would decrease the turnip output by a small amount, but because of the huge turnip surplus and the incredible shortage of all other foods that man-hour could produce a much greater benefit if devoted, let us say, to potatoes. The worker could be paid just as much for growing potatoes as turnips, and some lucky consumer would get the enormous benefit of variety in his diet. No one would be worse off, and at least one person would be better off; hence, the original situation, by our definition, could not have been efficient. Only when the world's resources were employed with a minimum of waste, expense, and unnecessary effort, and were employed producing the proper variety and diversity of goods and services in accordance with the law of diminishing marginal benefit would economic efficiency be attained.

But how do we know what is just the "proper" variety and diversity of goods and services? To answer this question we must apply what economists call the *equimarginal* principle. This principle has several aspects, some of which have been hinted at already. We saw before that I would be spending my lunch budget efficiently if I divided my money between coffee and donuts in such a way that the *marginal benefit* of a dime's worth of donuts would be *equal* to the *marginal benefit* of a dime's worth of coffee. If this principle were applied for each consumer and for all goods worldwide, one requirement for worldwide efficiency of resource allocation would be satisfied.

Another aspect of the equimarginal principle which must hold for efficient use of resources is that the marginal benefit to the consumer must equal the marginal cost to the producer for each item produced. The truth of this statement can be illustrated with a counter-example. If the lunch counter of the previous example can produce coffee at a marginal cost of four cents per cup, and I have to pay ten cents for it, an opportunity for mutual gain is being passed up. I will stop consumption, as we have already seen, when the marginal benefit to me of coffee falls to ten cents a cup, although I might be willing to pay as much as seven cents for still another. It is clear that if I made a special deal with the waitress and got a refill for five cents, I would get seven cents worth of benefit, the counter would get one cent worth of profit, and efficiency would be improved.

As an exercise the reader may wish to work out still another application of the equimarginal principle: Efficiency requires, when a given product is produced by two or more producers, that the marginal cost of production be the same for every producer.

The Invisible Hand

Making sure that the equimarginal principle is applied and that production and consumption are carried out efficiently on a world-wide scale is no mean trick. There are nearly four billion people in the world, most of them functioning in a dual role as producers and consumers, and heaven only knows how many hundreds of thousands or millions of separate and distinct goods and services are being produced. Applying the equimarginal principle on a world-wide scale, or even on a nationwide or citywide scale, necessarily requires an enormous network of communications and system of incentives. Communications are necessary, for how is one producer going to set his marginal cost equal to that of all others, or how is a consumer to buy eggs up to the point where marginal benefit declines to meet the marginal cost, or how are any of a number of other similar equimarginal conditions to be met, if all these quantities are not universally known? Yet communications alone is not enough, for what is to keep a producer from allowing his marginal cost to drift above or below the mark, or consumers to slip up with their marginal benefits, and so on, if each of these individuals does not have some incentive to pay attention to the proper quantities when they are communicated to him?

Various systems for maintaining communications and incentives could be imagined, and many have been tried – for example, providing communications by printing all the marginal costs and benefits in the newspaper every day, in tiny type like the stock market reports; and providing incentives by sending around a member of the King's Own Guard to beat up anyone who chose to ignore them. Or we could try having everyone send data on punchcards to the Central Statistical Agency, and solve the whole resource allocation problem on a giant computer, mailing a notice to each citizen with weekly production and consumption plans, and rewarding those who met the plans by placing a gold star beside their name on a chart at City Hall. Schemes like these have long been favored by all manner of utopians and social reformers and, with minor variations, many economies or at least parts of many economies in the world today are run according to principles of this general nature.

Other economies or parts of economies use a different type of communications and incentive mechanism known as the *competitive market*. In such an economy the chief means of communication is the price system. Since, as we saw above, the law of supply and demand in a competitive market tends to fix the price of a product at a level where marginal cost = price = marginal benefit, a knowledge of the prices of each product produced is all that a producer or consumer needs in order to apply the equimarginal principle if he so wishes. The incentive to do so comes, for the greedy Capitalistic producer, in the form of the profit motive-obeying the rule marginal cost = price will not only guarantee economic efficiency, about which the producer presumably cares not at all, but will also guarantee a maximum profit, for which he is presumably willing to slave day and night. For the consumer, equally indifferent to and even more likely ignorant of the principles of efficient resource allocation, the incentive to obey the equimarginal principle comes from the spur of necessity – unless his pay-check is bigger than mine, he will be very prudent in spending it to get the maximum possible benefit out of his limited budget, which he can do only by consciously or unconsciously equating the marginal benefits of the last penny's worth of each different good he consumes.

The eighteenth-century British economist Adam Smith was among the first to realize the efficiency with which the price system solved the problems of communication and incentives, of coordinating the selfish activities of producers and consumers to promote the socially desirable goal of rational resource allocation. Competition within the framework of the market economy seemed to him to be an "invisible hand" which, operating through the self-interest of the butcher and the baker and entirely without central calculation or control, supplied the populace with their daily bread and meat.

Cough, gasp! says the skeptical reader. If this invisible hand is so great, why can't it guide some self-interested soul to supply me with breathable air along with my meat and bread? And do I have to put up with that stinking cesspool of a river outside my window just because some invisible hand says I do? What about that SST that just flew overhead, did the invisible hand put that there, too? Or does the invisible hand need a big invisible handcuff if we are going to survive ecological disaster?

These are valid and challenging questions which the science of ecological economics must face. In reality, markets are not always perfect and don't always work. The price system does not always function smoothly, nor does it always lead to application of the equimarginal principle. A society is not necessarily desirable from every point of view just because it is efficient (although it is necessarily undesirable from any point of view if it is inefficient, taking the full definition of efficiency into account). It is so easy to find valid fault with the operation of the price system as it exists in the United States today that it is tempting to eliminate market mechanisms from consideration altogether as a means of coping with the environmental crisis.

In the following chapters, however, I will attempt time and again to make the point that the simple economic principles expounded by Adam Smith, elaborated by economists over the course of two hundred years, and presented here "in one easy lesson" can be ignored by would-be ecological reformers only at their peril. There is a lot of life left in the old invisible hand yet if we will just take the time to figure out how to put it to work.

Commentary

What has changed

The lesson of TANSTAAFL is that we can never escape the costs of living on a small planet. When we deplete high-quality deposits of non-renewable resources, we must bear the added costs of recycling or of turning to lower-quality deposits. When our production or consumption activities produce wastes, we must bear costs in the form of harm from pollution or the costs of pollution abatement and safe disposal. We can shift costs from one party to another, but we cannot make them go away. However, we can keep environmental costs from being higher than they need to be by following some well-established economic principles.

Consider the *equimarginal principle,* one of the central ideas in this chapter. Economists use the term *marginal* to refer to the costs or benefits of doing just a bit more of one thing or a bit less of another. For example, the benefit of spending one more dollar on pollution abatement can be called the *marginal benefit.* The equimarginal principle says that the total cost of pollution abatement will be minimized when an added dollar spent on abatement gives the same marginal benefit when spent controlling pollution from any one source as when spent on any other.

For example, suppose spending one more dollar reducing pollution from home heating turns out to have twice the benefit of spending one more dollar reducing pollution from cars. If that is true, we can achieve greater pollution abatement for any given level of spending by switching one dollar of abatement effort from cars to home heating. It will be worthwhile to continue doing so until diminishing returns bring the marginal benefits to an equal level.

The home heating example and similar examples spelled out in detail in the original chapter all focus on making the best use of scarce resources under known conditions of resource scarcities and technology. If I were rewriting the chapter today, I would be inclined to place greater emphasis on the equal importance of dealing with exploring new ways of doing things and adapting to change – changes in the physical environment, in peoples' preferences and demands, and in technology and organization. Those are areas of economics that receive special emphasis from writers of the Austrian school. In the long run, the best hope for achieving an environmentally sustainable economy requires more than just matching marginal costs and marginal benefits under static conditions. It also requires the talents of entrepreneurs in finding new ways of doing things, new technologies, and new methods of organizing production.

Fortunately, free markets, where they are allowed to operate, are good both at the short-run task of making the best use of resources and technologies available at the moment, and at the longer-run task of encouraging entrepreneurship and innovation. The truth of this statement, of course, depends on a correct understanding of what a "free market" is. A free market is not a "Drill baby, Drill!" paradise where businesses are free from government regulations, free to seek subsidies that loot the public treasury, and free to shift costs to anyone unlucky enough to live downstream or downwind. A market economy is not truly free unless it includes effective mechanisms to ensure that everyone, whether acting as producer, consumer, or agent of the government, respects the persons and property of others.

What has not changed

The ideas presented in this chapter were not new in 1971. Then, as now, they were familiar to anyone who had studied even a little economics. That has not changed. Sadly, however well-established the economic principles are they remain widely ignored when it comes to designing policies.

Fuel economy standards for automobiles, for decades a centerpiece of U.S. energy policy, are a case in point. Suppose we want to achieve a given reduction, say 100 million gallons a month, in the total amount of gasoline consumed by the U.S. auto fleet. How can we reach that target at the minimum cost? Clearly, one thing needed is to follow the equimarginal principle. That would require, among other things, that an added dollar invested in improving the fuel economy of a given car yields the same reduction in total fuel consumption as a dollar invested in any other car.

The problem with fuel economy standards is that they violate precisely that fundamental principle. Among other things, they ignore the fact that some cars are used differently than others. Following the equimarginal principle would require investing more in improving the fuel economy of cars that are driven many miles a year, and less in those that are driven few miles, rather than focusing on improvement in the average fuel economy of the fleet of cars produced by each manufacturer.

Unfortunately, government regulators cannot know how many miles a given car will be driven. Only the owner is likely to have that information. What we need, then, is a policy that gives owners an incentive to spend more on fuel economy features when they buy a car they plan to drive a lot, and at the same time, gives them an incentive to drive fewer miles in cars that do not have as many fuel economy features.

What kind of policy would do that? Any policy that enlisted the price system would work better than the command-and-control approach embodied in fuel economy standards. For example, one simple approach would be to increase the federal gasoline tax. If gas cost more at the pump, people would have just the right incentive to make the optimal investments. People who drove many miles per year would be willing to spend more than they do now to buy vehicles engineered for greater fuel efficiency. People who drove only a few miles would spend less, buying simple, cheap cars that did not get such good mileage. People who found themselves with both a high-mileage and a low-mileage vehicle in their garage would drive the high-mileage one more often and save the low-mileage one for uses where its special characteristics, perhaps the ability to carry a large load, were really needed. The tax could be adjusted up or down until any given target for fuel saving was met for the whole country. The total cost of reaching the target would be much less than when the same amount was invested in each car regardless of how much it was driven.

Using the price mechanism would have another payoff, beyond that of promoting efficiency under given technology. A high fuel price would mean big rewards for any entrepreneur who could bring out a car that cost less to build or gave a better driving experience for the amount of fuel it used. Higher gas prices would surely accelerate the introduction of plug-in hybrids, all-electric vehicles, and kits for converting cars to run on compressed natural gas. They would also give consumers an incentive to find new ways of economizing on fuel, say, by moving closer to work or using public transportation.

What objection could conceivably be raised to a gas tax, if it would achieve the same environmental objective as fuel economy standards, but at a lower cost? No objection, if you are an economist. But if you are a politician, the gas tax has an obvious drawback: it makes the cost of reducing fuel consumption highly visible. You see the big dollars-per-gallon number right there in front of you every time you drive up to the pump. Fuel economy standards, on the other hand, hide the cost. You pay the price of a higher-mileage car only now and then, when you buy a new car, and even then, the part of the price attributable to the mileage-enhancing features is not broken out as a separate item on the sticker. You may notice that your new car costs more than your old one did, but there are lots of other reasons for that besides fuel economy.

It is a classic case of the TANSTAAFL principle – if you try to make something look like it's free, it only ends up costing more in the long run. If you are a politician, you may well prefer a big hidden cost to a small visible cost. But if you are a friend of our planet, you should know better than to be suckered by the promise of a free lunch.

Chapter 3
POLLUTION AND THE PRICE SYSTEM

The Invisible Hand Slips Up

The first thing which comes to mind for most people, when they think of the environmental crisis, is pollution. The population explosion, the disappearance of the wilderness, the exhaustion of the world's supply of oil and copper ore, imminent though some say they are, seem remote by comparison. Today *The New York Times* can print a map showing an ominous black splotch, representing the danger area with more than 10 parts per million of sulfur dioxide in the air spreading over most of Manhattan. The death of Lake Erie and the famous Cuyahoga River fire are almost matters of ancient history. Even in pastoral Vermont, the number of different shots needed before diving in at the local swimming hole serves as a reminder that no place is safe. As far away as the Antarctic, the penguins are said to have DDT in their blood. Is all this the unavoidable price of progress with which we must simply learn to live? The answer to this question is partly yes, but mostly no.

It is partly yes, because of the TANSTAAFL principle. Everything good has a price, and that includes a price for clean air, clean water, virgin forests, and quiet streets. We can have a little more of this only at the expense of a little less of that, and only the addict will choose to expend all of his resources on one item without regard for the alternatives foregone. Surely most of us would permit a few trees to be cut down to prevent the monotony of row upon row of cinderblock houses and room upon room of plastic furniture. We would consider tolerating the exhaust of a few cars and planes rather than live the stultifying life of a man who never travels beyond the confines of the county where he was born. A world totally without pollution, a world in which all of nature was labeled "Iook, don't touch" would be too poor in other things to be the object of our aspirations.

But although for most of us the best of all possible worlds would contain some nonzero degree of pollution, it does not necessarily mean that our market economy gives us just the right amount. It does not do so, and would not, in fact, even if it were a perfectly functioning market free of all the problems of monopolies, immobilities, ignorance, dysfunctional traditions and prejudices, and so on which beset the real world. From the point of view of ecological economics the basic flaw in the theory of the efficient, self-regulating market economy is that the price system, as it currently exists, is suitable for use only in the throughput economy. As soon as we develop an awareness that we are living not in a throughput economy but aboard the spaceship earth, we can begin to see that Adam Smith's invisible hand is no longer so reliable as we once thought.

To see why this is so, let us look at a simple example. Figure 3.1 is a map showing the location of industry along the banks of a certain river. Along the higher reaches several paper mills are located. These produce, along with paper, quite a bit of waste material, which is dumped directly into the river. Somewhat farther downstream there is a water works, which draws water from the river and purifies it to serve the needs of a small town located nearby.

An investigation of the economics of paper production and water purification reveals the following situation: The paper mills, taken together, are producing 10 tons of paper per day. The mill owners have found that an additional dollar spent on the production of paper (properly allocated to the purchase of additional labor, machinery, and raw materials) will give an increase in output of 200 pounds. Our investigation further reveals that these paper mills are competitive profit maximizers, as good Capitalist firms should be, and are thus selling their product at a price of 1/2 cent per pound, just equal to marginal cost. Down at the water works, the cost situation is slightly more complicated. The chief engineer knows that the basic cost of pumping water from the river and filtering out the natural sediments is a constant 50 cents per 1,000 gallons. However, the effluent from the paper mills complicates the water purification process. In fact, for each ton of paper produced, it is necessary to spend an extra five cents per 1,000 gallons on additional filtration and chemical treatment of the river water before it becomes fit to drink. At the moment, then, with paper output at ten tons per day, the cost of water is one dollar per thousand gallons. The water works is not a competitive firm, but a wise economist on the city council has decreed that water should be sold at marginal cost anyhow. At the price of a dollar per 1,000 gallons, 100,000 gallons of water are sold each day in the community.

The consumers in this town, like consumers everywhere, are interested in spending their limited budgets on paper and water in such a way as to get a maximum of satisfaction. Finding water available at 1/10 of a cent per gallon and paper at 1/2 cent per pound, they adjust their consumption of the two products until the satisfaction they would get from an additional pound of paper is just equal to that which would be yielded by 5 more gallons of water.

From our previous discussion we might be tempted to conclude that the situation just described would be a classic example of efficient allocation of resources via the market. When producers sell their product at marginal cost, and consumers adjust their consumption to equate the marginal benefit of a penny's worth of each product, the equimarginal principle is satisfied – or has something been left out? Let us check to see whether our previous reasoning remains valid when dealing with an economic situation in which the throughput assumption is violated, as it is in this case by the existence of the environmental feedback link of the river which serves simultaneously as a pollutable sink for the paper mill and as an exploitable source for the water works.

In order for resources to be allocated efficiently, as we saw above, consumers must pursue each line of consumption exactly to the point where the marginal benefit of an additional unit expenditure exactly balances the marginal benefit of the opportunities foregone. Where only the two goods, water and paper, exist this rule means that paper must be consumed to the point where the benefit yielded by an additional penny's worth (2 pounds) of paper just equals the benefit which would be yielded by the quantity of water which must be sacrificed in order to obtain that 2 pounds of paper.

This is just where the catch comes in. In the market the consumers, ignorant of the technology of paper and water production, must depend on the price system to tell them how much water must be foregone to get 2 pounds of paper. The answer given by the price system is 5 gallons. Despite the fact that the prices of both paper and water are equal to their marginal costs, this is the wrong answer.

To answer the question of how much water must be given up to gain a pound of paper correctly, let us perform a simple experiment. Shift $1.00 worth of productive resources out of the production of water and put them to work in one of the paper mills. Since the marginal cost of water is 1/10 cent per gallon, we know that diverting the dollar's worth of resources from the water works will cause a drop in output of 1000 gallons, leaving a total output of 99,000 gallons per day. Since the marginal cost of paper is 1/2 cent per pound, this same unit of resources will be capable of adding 200 pounds per day to the output of the paper mill, where it is put to work. The immediate result of the resource shift is to exchange 1,000 gallons of water for 200 pounds of paper, a 5:1 ratio just equal to the ratio of marginal costs, the price ratio, and the consumers' marginal benefit ratio.

However, we cannot leave things at that. So far we have not taken into account the effect of the environmental link between paper and water production. A few hours or a few days after this initial resource shift has been made, the effect will begin to be noticed down at the water works, for the 200 pound step up in paper production will result in a proportionate increase in effluent discharge upstream. Since each ton of paper production adds 5 cents to the cost of water purification, we know that the cost of water purification will go up exactly from $1.00 to $1.005, or by 0.5 percent. This additional cost means that the $99 worth of resources left at the water works can no longer process the same amount of water as before. In fact, output at the water works will drop by approximately an additional 500 gallons to 98,500 gallons. Our conclusion must be that the extra 200 pounds of paper which were gained by the transfer of a dollar's worth of resources required the sacrifice not of 1,000 gallons but of 1,500 gallons of water, half again as much as we would have predicted from looking at the price ratio!

Figure 3.1 Map

PAPER MILLS

WATER WORKS

This means that the economy is not giving the consumers in town the greatest possible satisfaction from the productive resources which they are paying to have employed in the two lines of production. Consumers misled by market prices into thinking they must forego only 5 gallons of water to gain a pound of paper, demand relatively too much paper. If they knew that the benefit foregone was that of 7-1/2 gallons of water, they would switch their consumption patterns in favor of water. Workers would be laid off in the paper mills and taken on in the water works until the falling marginal benefit of water and the rising marginal benefit of paper were brought into the 7-1/2 to 1 ratio. Then, and only then, would the equimarginal principle be satisfied.

If an economy is inefficient, as this one was before we came upon the scene, it will always be possible to draw up some sort of a contract or agreement which would be voluntarily acceptable by all participants in the economy, that is, which would benefit at least one of them without making any of them worse off. In the case under discussion .the possibility for such an agreement does exist.[15] For example, we might propose a multilateral contract which would be signed 1. by all consumers in the community (say there are 200 of them) who would each agree to buy 1 pound less of paper and in return receive a special coupon entitling them to buy 6 gallons of water for the price which they would normally have to pay for 5; 2. by the 5 paper mill owners, who would each agree to release 20 cents worth of resources from the production of paper and in return get 10 free gallons of water; and 3. by the director of the water works, who would agree to spend $1.00 more on the purification of water provided that the other parties kept their parts of the bargain. It is clear that each group would profit from this. The consumers, who had previously adjusted their paper and water purchases to the point where they placed equal value on 1 pound of paper and 5 gallons of water would be getting a bonus of 1 gallon above and beyond the bare minimum 5 gallons, which they would accept in

---

15 The reader should be cautioned that the significance of the agreement proposed here is primarily theoretical rather than practical. See Chapter 4 below.

exchange for giving up 1 pound of paper. The paper producer would lose 40 pounds of paper production, and hence 20 cents in revenue, by cutting back his productive expenditures 20 cents, but would be compensated by the bonus of 10 gallons of free water, which he could use himself or sell at the market price. The director of the water works would incur an increase in costs of $1.00 but because of the reduction in pollution would gain from the deal not 1,000 but 1,500 gallons of added production. He would make back his added costs on the 1,200 gallons which he sold to consumers at the reduced price of 1/12 cent per gallon, would give away 50 gallons free to the mill owners in that part of the bargain, and would be left with 250 gallons surplus to be sold at a profit.

It is hoped that this example will provide a sufficient intuitive base for three generalizations, the rigorous proof of which would be too complex to enter into here. All of these generalizations concern a distinction between internal and external costs. By internal costs, we mean the value of resources used up directly in an act of production and consumption by the person doing the producing or consuming. By external costs, we mean the value of resources which are used up indirectly or inadvertently as a by-product of the act of production or consumption. (In the example which we have just discussed, the production of paper involved internal costs of 1/2 cent per pound, representing the value of the labor, machinery, and raw materials used up internally within the paper mill; and external costs of 1/4 cent per pound, representing the value of the labor, filtration devices, and chemicals which were used downstream in the water works to counteract the additional pollution of the water caused by the production of that pound of paper.)

The distinction between internal and external costs may be expressed in several other ways and seen in many other examples. For instance, we could distinguish internal costs as those which are imposed upon the person who initiates and directly benefits from the activity in question, and external costs as those which he imposes upon others. Consider a person who operates a noisy motorcycle. He himself bears the costs of gasoline, maintenance, depreciation, and so forth; but he succeeds in imposing part of the costs of operation on others when instead of spending money for a quieter muffler he makes others pay for soundproofing, tranquilizers, and sleeping pills – or just pay in nervous energy.

Another way to look at the distinction is to say that internal costs correspond to voluntary transactions, while external costs correspond to involuntary, forced transactions. When I buy a bottle of beer I engage in a voluntary transaction with the storekeeper, a two-way exchange in which I give him some money and he gives me the bottle. When I throw the empty bottle out of my car window onto your lawn I am forcing you to participate in a one-way, involuntary transaction – you give me the service of rubbish disposal, whether you want to or not, and I give you nothing in return.

Finally, we could classify as internal costs those which use up resources by setting in motion a chain of cause and effect which travels through the market system, and external costs as those which use up resources by setting off chains of cause and effect passing through the natural environment. When a farmer sprays his apple trees, he sets off chain reactions of both types. He uses the retailing services of his local supplier, who in turn uses the wholesale services of regional suppliers, who in turn draws on the productive capacity of a chemical plant, which in turn uses up labor and raw materials, the production of which necessitates the use of still other resources, and so on. The price of the insecticide represents the sum total of all the costs added up all along the line, and the farmer pays this as an internal cost of producing apples. But the use of pesticides also sets off other chains of cause and effect – the material washes off his trees into nearby streams, where it is eaten by little fish who concentrate it in their fatty tissues, and in turn swim downstream to be eaten by bigger fish who further concentrate the poison. These bigger fish are eaten by, among other creatures, the American bald eagle, who consequently lays eggs with soft shells or no shells at all, and is thus threatened with extinction. How much is an eagle worth? A man who illegally shoots one must pay a $500 fine for the privilege, but a farmer who poisons one as part of the external costs of growing apples pays nothing.

Now we come to the three generalizations concerning internal and external costs which were promised earlier. The first of these is that whenever external costs of production or consumption are present in an economy, the invisible hand of competition will, if unaided, fail as a guide to the efficient allocation of resources.

The second generalization, really a corollary of the first, is that whenever external effects of production or consumption exist, there will in principle exist some potential agreement among all parties concerned which will benefit at least one person and harm none of the others. This means, among other things, that whenever the external cost in question is a form of pollution, there exists some possible pollution abatement program benefiting both the perpetrator and the victims of the pollution.

The third generalization is that whenever an activity involves pollution, or the imposition of some other type of external cost, a reduction in that activity will almost always be part of any program to achieve an efficient allocation of the resources involved. If the production of steel, cement, or automobile transportation pollutes the air, we may be pretty sure that we should be using less of these and more, say, of aluminum, bricks, and electric railways.

How to Make Pollution Go Away

If pollution is such an indisputably bad thing, the reader may say, not only unpleasant and aesthetically offensive but inefficient and harmful to polluter and victim alike, then let's just get rid of it! Let's get the government to ban leaded gasoline, outlaw DDT, regulate the type of fuel used by Con Ed, require secondary treatment for all sewage, impose standards on atomic power stations, insist on chemical toilets on all pleasure boats, punish people who litter the highways, and control the phosphate content of detergents! After all, isn't that what the government is for – to ban, outlaw, regulate, require, impose, insist, punish, and control?

This seems to be the instinctive reaction of a great many Americans upset about the pollution problem. The politicians whom they send to our legislatures at regularly appointed intervals are only too happy to oblige – if this new public concern will give them a chance to control something which they do not yet control, or set up a bureau or regulatory commission where one does not yet exist, what intelligent politician would pass up the opportunity?

To succumb to the urge to control pollution via the imposition of direct controls out of the belief that these are quick, expedient, or effective ways of getting the job done, would, I believe, be a grave mistake. Instead, I would like to offer some guidelines for a more efficient, equitable, and effective pollution abatement policy.

The first guideline which I propose is to make minimum use of direct controls in fighting pollution, and maximum use of market mechanisms and the price system. To illustrate how this guideline might be applied in a specific case let us take the very important example of automobile exhaust pollution. This is, incidentally, an area in which direct controls are already being used in the form of requiring certain emission control devices on all cars produced in and imported into the United States. Other direct controls are pending, including regulation of permissible types of fuels, still more effective emission control devices, and the outright banning of automobile traffic from certain urban areas.

As an alternative to such proposals, I would argue in favor of controlling auto exhaust pollution by putting a price tag on the privilege to pollute. In our Capitalist economy you can impose upon me the inconvenience of work or the inconvenience of using my lawn as a parking lot only by paying a price, and if I do not judge the price to be high enough I am free to decline your offer. Why, then, should you be able to impose upon me the inconvenience of breathing the noxious gases emitted from your exhaust pipe without paying a price, when, because of the simple physics of the situation, I don't even have the opportunity to refuse your offer to have me breathe them?

The idea of putting a price on exhaust emission at first may bring to mind the image of a little gadget like a water meter which would be clamped on the tailpipe of a car to be read once a month and a bill sent out, so much per cubic foot. If the construction of such a meter were practical, it would be an ideal method to use. As far as I know, this meter has not yet been developed, but a somewhat more primitive approach using existing institutions and technology could accomplish much the same purpose. For example, in a state like Vermont, which already requires a semiannual trip to the inspection station, the pollution charge could be combined with regular inspection. When a car was taken in, it would be rated according to an established scale of points. Starting with a basic score scaled to the engine displacement and mileage since the last inspection, so many points could be deducted for a P.C.V. system, and so many points for fuel injection, a catalytic muffler, and so on and so forth. At the end, a fee would be paid in proportion to the points remaining, which might range, let us imagine, from $100 for a massive Chrysler with no technical refinements down to $2.00 for a Volkswagen converted to run on natural gas.

Compared to the current system of direct controls, the price system would offer distinct advantages with respect to efficiency, equity, and incentives. Let us look at these advantages one by one.

The price system would be more efficient because it would observe the equimarginal principle. If you are going to use up resources in a variety of related but not identical activities, you will get the greatest yield per unit expenditure by dividing your resources among the different activities in such a way that the benefit of spending an additional penny at the margin is the same for each activity.

This principle applies also to the control of automobile exhaust. The total amount of pollution control expenditure should be divided among individual cars in such a way that the marginal yield, measured in terms, say, of cubic feet of carbon monoxide reduction per dollar spent, would be the same for all cars.

Now, direct controls clearly violate this principle. The current law requires that some fixed sum – let us say about $10.00 – be spent on every car for positive crankcase ventilation. In the case of a big car which is driven a lot, that $10.00 does a great deal of good. In the case of a little car, or a little used one, it does less good. Clearly, it would be more efficient to spend some of the money used on the little cars for still better control devices on big cars. Under the price system this would be done. A Buick-owning traveling salesman would probably get almost every device in the book before he got to the point where another dollar spent on technical refinements would not pay off in terms of reduced inspection tax, while the proverbial little old lady who drives her Renault once a week to church might find that even the most basic devices weren't worth putting on.

The second point of superiority of the price system lies in its equity. This has already been hinted at in our previous example – it is clearly equitable that the salesman pay more pollution tax than the little old lady. In addition to this aspect of equity, which makes people pay in proportion to the cost which they impose on others by pollution, there is another, almost reverse aspect. It is also equitable to allow people to pollute more in proportion to the benefit which they gain from pollution! Compare two car owners, one of whom views his car just as a means of getting from place to place and the other for whom his car is his principle hobby and driving his chief source of amusement. The first man will be little inconvenienced by the slight reduction in performance which is produced by the mandatory P.C.V. system. The second man, however, will be grievously annoyed when he finds that his zero-to-sixty acceleration time has risen from 9.6 seconds to 9.7. Would it not be more equitable to allow this second man to take his P.C.V. valve off, as long as he is willing to pay the increased inspection tax which will result and as long as that tax realistically reflects the cost which he imposes upon others by so doing?

Finally, the price system for exhaust emission control would be superior to the direct control system with respect to its incentive value. This must already be clear in general terms, but let us add a few specifics. It must be pointed out that under the current system there is no incentive whatsoever for the car owner to maintain pollution control devices installed by law on his car. Here we are not just worried about the hot rodder who purposely takes the thing off to get that extra edge of performance. More significantly, how many car owners even know that the Rochester valve of the P.C.V. system must be replaced every 10,000 miles or the system is rendered useless? And of those who do know this, how many are tempted to save the dollar or two a year involved by just letting the matter slide?

Furthermore, in the matter of incentives it is not so much the car owner as the car manufacturer who counts. The present system by insisting that every car maker, domestic and foreign, be treated exactly equally guarantees that no manufacturer can get a competitive advantage by producing a more pollution-free car. In fact, the situation is if anything the exact opposite. If the manufacturer is going to act rationally in his own self-interest to maximize his profits, it will pay him to spend millions not in the research laboratories but in the lobbies of Congress fighting pollution control legislation tooth and nail! There is much talk about a "conspiracy" of the big three to suppress technical developments which could reduce pollution. Maybe there is a conspiracy and maybe there isn't, but how long do you think one could last against the competition of Volkswagen, Fiat, and Toyota if the annual pollution charge paid by the owner for an American car was triple that for their foreign competitors? Let's take the profit out of pollution and put it into pollution control, then we'll get a real look at the Capitalist economy in action.

There are a few signs on the horizon that the price system for pollution control may be gaining favor. For automobiles, President Nixon's tax on the lead additive in gasoline appears to be a small step in the right general direction. The system has been widely suggested for control of water pollution also, where the metering of wastes is more practical. A similar system is already in use in the Ruhr Valley in Germany, and pilot programs are underway in this country. The possibilities have still not been fully explored. How about, for example, a differential charge for garbage collection in the city according to whether noisy metal cans or quiet plastic ones are used? How about a differential liquor tax on beer according to whether the product is sold in indestructible aluminum cans or biodegradable plastic containers?

All of the pricing schemes mentioned so far have one drawback in common in that they require initiative to be taken by the government to put them into effect, and administration and regulation by bureaucratic government agencies. As long as cleaning up pollution is left to the politicians there is grave danger that whatever Federal Pollution Control Commission is set up will go the way of the FCC, the FDA, the ICC, the CAB, and virtually all other federal, state, and local regulatory and licensing agencies. In case after case the ordinary citizen has seen that regulators quickly become tools of those whom they supposedly regulate. Corruption and the protection of special interests creep in, and public service drops to last priority.

For this reason, I will propose a second guideline, namely that whenever possible the price system for pollution control should be instituted not by administrative means but by modifications of our legal system and the extension of the property rights of individuals.

Property rights are a part of our social system which, if they are to be justified at all, must be justified on the grounds that they induce socially beneficial behavior. Our private property system in this country, like almost all other aspects of our economic system, was developed in the 19th century, a time when, at least in the wide-open continent of America, the throughput economy model was not such a wildly inaccurate picture of the world as it is today. In the throughput economy of the 19th century the most important socially beneficial behavior which was stimulated by the private property system was the function of asset creation (capital formation, saving, or whatever you want to call it) that led to economic growth. Now that we live in the spaceship earth of the late 20th century we know that the path to the good life no longer lies through the brute force method of asset creation alone. Instead, we must learn to economize on the use of sources and sinks which we once thought limitless, and learn to recycle our wastes. What is the matter with our laws and property rights, and how can they be modified to suit the new conditions? I will give just two examples.

In the first, let us look at water pollution again. A great American industrialist is reputed to have said that the ability of our rivers and streams to carry sewage off to the ocean is one of our great natural resources. He couldn't have been more correct! These great natural sewers must surely have contributed as much to American economic development as our vast ore and coal fields, the great wheat lands, or the forests of the Northwest. But the exploitation of timber, cropland, and mineral rights, although undergoing some terribly wasteful phases in the last century when these were treated virtually as free goods, has now been brought under fairly rational control by the simple fact that each unit of these resources is the private property of some individual or business corporation. If you want to cut down a tree, you are going to have to pay the owner, so you don't do it unless you really need that wood and can't use a substitute. The same goes for corn, steel, oil, or anything else. Yet our great natural sewers are the property of no one! Since no one has any property rights in them, who is going to guard against their destruction? Who is going to charge for their use? Small wonder we are a hundred years behind on water pollution control.

What could be done to save the situation within the framework of the property system? A really radical proposal would be for the federal government to put all the nation's major rivers and lakes up for auction, and let the highest bidders regulate and economize on their use. If General Motors owned the Mississippi River, it would surely charge for the privilege of dumping in it, and would presumably also consider bids for conservation groups and communities to keep parts of it clean for bathing and fishing.

A less radical proposal than actually creating property rights in the rivers would be to create property rights in the right to pollute itself. It has been suggested that the government auction off a certain number of certificates, fixed once and for all, each giving the right to dump so many thousands of cubic feet of waste. These certificates would then become the property of their owners, to be bought and sold at will. They would end up in the hands of those industries where pollution control was most technically difficult and expensive, and other industries would move or clean up rather than pay the price of a certificate.

The second example for pollution control via the law of property has to do with the obscure corner of the legal system known as the law of nuisance. In our system property ownership includes the right to use free from outside interference, as well as the obligation to use in such a way as not to injure others. Unfortunately, our system for enforcing the first right is faulty. Our laws work pretty well in the area of private nuisance. If you build a barbeque in your back yard, and the smoke blows over and ruins the flavor of the cupcakes baked in the bakery next door, chances are you will be sued and have to pay damages. These damage payments, or the threat of them, put a price on pollution for you and deter you from building the barbeque or using it as often as you otherwise would.

In the area of law known as public nuisance, however, the system does not work nearly as well. If the previous example is changed so that you are building a steel mill, and causing damage not only to your neighbor but to all the inhabitants of a forty-mile radius, you might imagine that the threat of suit and the imposition of damages would be still greater than before. But it is less! This is because only an agency of the government is empowered to sue for public nuisance. An individual cannot initiate a suit unless he can show special damages concentrated upon him alone (for example, the bakery might be able to sue the steel mill). It is as if the law allowed you to defend yourself against a mugger who attacked only you, but did nothing to help if he robbed just a little from everyone in your neighborhood!

The problem is very similar to that in some areas of consumer protection law. If General Motors builds a defective car an individual can, under the proper conditions, sue the company to recover damages to himself. A few such cases will do little to compel the company to build safer cars, since the damages in each case will be small. To solve the problem it has been suggested that the law be modified to allow an individual to bring what is called a "class suit," a suit requiring payment of damages to himself and to all others similarly damaged, however many thousands of these there may be. The threat of class suits, it is hoped, will deter companies from making shoddy products.

The class suit principle could also be brought to bear in the area of pollution, by modifying the law to allow an individual to bring a class suit against the perpetrator of a public nuisance. This would be an enormously powerful deterrent to industrial pollution. Imagine that just one of the residents of the lower stretches of a river were able to bring a suit against a large polluter upstream for the total sum of damages to all residents! This would certainly put a high price tag on pollution and the company would be forced to shut down, clean up, or compensate the damaged parties for the violation of their property rights.

As in the case of emission and effluent charges there are a few hopeful signs of progress in reforming the legal system to help control pollution. The State of Michigan, for example, has recently passed and signed into law a measure that will allow a citizen to file suit against anyone, including the state itself, believed to be seriously contaminating the air, water, or land resources belonging to all. This is obviously a step in the right direction. It has the drawback, from the economist's point of view, of not providing for the payment of damages to injured parties but only permitting the court to grant injunctions, impose conditions, or direct the upgrading of standards for the polluter, and thus of simply transferring the problems of direct controls from the executive to the judicial branches of government. Nonetheless, it has the enormous advantage of allowing the injured party, the private citizen, to take the initiative against major polluters without being subject to the quick brush-off or the endless delay which are the twin traits of administrative bureaucracy.

Commentary

What has changed

Climate change moves to center stage

The biggest single change since this chapter was written is the emergence of climate change as the central environmental issue of our time.

In part, climate change has moved to center stage because real progress has been made in dealing with some of the other kinds of pollution that dominated the debate in the 1970s. For example, when I was writing the 1971 edition, I was living on the banks of the White River in Vermont. At that time many towns were still dumping untreated sewage in the river, so by midsummer, as water levels dropped, we had to stop using our favorite swimming hole. Just twenty years later, cleanup had progressed to the point that you could swim all summer long. Over the same time span, the number of Stage 1 smog alert days in Los Angeles dropped from over a hundred per year to single digits in some years. Along the way, lead disappeared from our gasoline, ozone-destroying chlorofluorocarbons disappeared from our hair spray, and the DDT-threatened eagle made a gratifying comeback.

In part also, climate change has become a bigger issue because it has become more obvious that it is happening. Nine of the first ten years of the 21st century have made the all-time ten-warmest list. CO_2 concentrations in the atmosphere, a key driver of climate change, have increased from under 330 in 1971 to over 390 in 2011. There are still plenty of unbelievers around, but numbers like those just cited have gotten the attention of the environmentalist community. Every year brings the news that another prominent climate-change skeptic has switched sides. I have never heard of a serious climate scientist or economist making the switch the other way. The most prominent remaining skeptics are candidates for public office who make a political strategy out of denying rather than confronting inconvenient truths.

In some ways, climate change strengthens the central argument of this chapter, which is that we can enlist the price system to help control pollution. Tailpipe emissions from automobiles are a case in point. The focus of the original version of this chapter was on emissions that produce local smog, such as carbon monoxide, ozone and oxides of nitrogen. The idea of putting a price on those pollutants raised some tricky measurement questions. First, there was the purely technical one of how to measure the stuff coming out of your tailpipe. There was no practical metering device available at the time to measure them car-by-car in real time, and as far as I know, there still is not. Furthermore, a given amount of ozone emitted in downtown Los Angeles clearly does more harm than the same amount emitted on a rural road in Idaho, so a single, national pollution charge would not have been appropriate.

Given those problems, implementing a pay-for-pollution scheme would have had to rely on some formula that used proxy variables such as engine displacement, miles driven per year, and the zip code where a vehicle was registered. Such a formula would never more than approximate the pollution damage done by the vehicle, and it would be hard to administer. Its complexity, like that of the U.S. tax code, would induce clever methods of evasion, some within the letter of the law and some not.

By comparison, imposing a price on automotive emissions of CO_2 is simple. All you have to do is add the price of pollution into the price of fuel at the pump. True, the exact damage per ton of carbon emitted is in dispute, but at least there is no argument about how much carbon there is in a gallon of gasoline. Pick a good damage estimate, say $100 per ton of carbon. Convert it to cents per gallon (each $10 per ton of carbon works out to about ten cents per gallon), and add it to the existing federal gasoline tax. Adjust the tax appropriately for lower-carbon fuels like compressed natural gas. It doesn't make any difference where emissions take place, since all CO_2 everywhere pours into the same global airshed.

In other ways, though, climate change is a more difficult problem than local air pollution. Damage estimates are subject to a high degree of uncertainty. All sources of carbon should, ideally, be treated equally, whether they come from transportation, industry, or farming, but different mechanisms might have to be used to impose the charge in each case. Various greenhouse gasses like methane and nitrous oxide would have to be converted to CO_2 equivalents and included in the scheme. Furthermore, a really effective pay-for-pollution scheme would have to be implemented, if not everywhere, at least in all major industrial countries.

It may prove impossible to develop an effective worldwide policy to mitigate climate change. That does not mean we will escape paying for the effects of climate change, however. It only means that we will be paying the costs of adapting to climate change rather than avoiding it, costs that may well be higher in the long run.

Experience with pay-for-pollution

Another change since 1971 is the accumulation of practical experience with pay-for-pollution policies, of which this chapter discussed three variants. The first approach is for people to defend their property and persons against pollution using tort law. Libertarian purists consider this the true free market approach. The other two approaches institute pay-for-pollution mechanisms through government regulation: Emission charges (or pollution taxes, if you prefer that term), and tradable pollution permits (now widely known as cap-and-trade).

The most important policy initiatives of the past 40 years have taken the cap-and-trade approach. The cap is a fixed maximum level of pollution, lower than the prevailing level. To implement the cap, regulators issue an appropriate quantity of permits, each allowing a certain number of units of pollution. The permits can initially be "grandfathered" (distributed free-of-charge to existing sources in proportion to the pollution they produce) or they can be sold at auction. Once in the hands of the public, the permits are traded on an organized exchange at a price determined by supply and demand. Firms that can control emissions at a relatively low cost become sellers of permits and those with higher control costs become buyers. In that way, the equimarginal principle is served, and emissions are brought down to the target level in a cost-effective manner.

The first large-scale cap-and-trade program in the United States was introduced, in the 1990s, to control sulfur dioxide (SO_2) emissions. SO_2 pollution, mainly from power plants and other coal-burning industrial sources, along with related gasses like oxides of nitrogen, were increasing the acidity of rain in downwind locations. The acid rain, in turn, was causing widespread damage to forests, lakes, farms, and even urban buildings.

Initially, the idea of tradable SO_2 permits met with resistance. Industries argued that permit prices would rise to astronomical levels, threatening some polluters with bankruptcy. Conservationists derided the policy as a "pollute-and-pay" regime that would allow power plants and other sources to continue business as usual while paying token fees.

Both sides were proved wrong. Permit prices were high enough to encourage substantial emission reductions, but not so high as to drive firms out of business. By the early 2000s, acid rain intensity in the northeastern United States had dropped to half of its peak level. SO_2 permit trading was being called the greatest environmental policy success story of recent times.

Unfortunately, in 2010, the great success story collapsed in a heap. Although it had operated successfully for many years, its complexity left it open to legal challenges. In response to adverse court decisions, the Environmental Protection Agency changed the rules of the game in ways that caused outstanding permits to become worthless. Some sources, including some categories of coal-fired power plants, were subjected to new command-and-control rules requiring greater emission reductions than those achieved under permit trading. At the same time, other sources lost all incentive to reduce emissions, since the permits they could earn by doing so no longer had any market value. It is too early to know what the long-run impact will be on acid rain levels, but there is no doubt that the whole episode is a setback for the cap-and-trade concept.

Meanwhile, a second major cap-and-trade initiative was undertaken, this one in Europe. In 2005, as part of its effort to comply with the Kyoto climate change protocol, the European Union introduced an ambitious emissions trading system (EU ETS) for carbon dioxide.

EU ETS remains the largest pay-for-pollution scheme in operation, but it, too, has experienced problems. At first, too many permits were issued, causing their market price to fall close to zero. After quotas were tightened, permit prices rose to over €20 per ton, but they fell sharply again after the 2008 financial crisis. Price volatility has undermined the hope that permit trading would provide a clear framework of expectations for investments in low-emission technologies.

Another problem with EU ETS has been "leakage" of emissions outside the EU – a tendency to move emission-intensive activities to countries where they are less strictly regulated. Leakage was supposed to be controlled by the possibility of earning credits for emission-control activities in developing countries, but that part of the scheme has not worked well. Difficulty in measuring emission reductions elsewhere in the world, and sometimes outright fraud, have allowed European companies to receive emission credits for projects in China or India when there was little or no real reduction in global greenhouse gas emissions. Furthermore, it has proved politically difficult to extend the scope of EU ETS beyond the energy and heavy industrial sectors, which account for just 40 percent of total emissions. On the whole, EU ETS has been only a qualified success.

Back in the United States, hopes for cap-and-trade reached a new high during the 2008 presidential elections, when both the Republican candidate, John McCain, and the Democrat, Barack Obama, officially endorsed the concept. Bipartisan support did not prove durable, however. In 2009, the House of Representatives managed to pass an emissions-trading bill, American Clean Energy and Security Act (ACES, also known as Waxman-Markey), but the bill attracted only 8 Republican votes. In the Senate, despite a Democratic majority, backers of the bill could not put together the 60 votes needed to break a Republican filibuster. (We will return to the reasons for this failure in the next chapter.) In the same year, attempts at the 2009 Copenhagen climate summit to achieve a worldwide cap-and-trade system for carbon emissions also failed.

On balance, the collapse of SO_2 trading, the death of Waxman-Markey, and the qualified success of EU ETS add up to two-and-a-half strikes against emission trading. Partly because of the political problems of emission trading, and partly on theoretical grounds, economists today are more likely to favor emission charges as the most promising approach to implementing the pay-for-pollution concept. However, both cap-and-trade and emissions charges run into opposition on grounds discussed in the next section.

What has not changed

One thing that has not changed much since 1971 is widespread political opposition to putting a price on pollution. Opponents rarely dispute the logic of externalities and efficiency that make such policies appealing to economists. Instead, the resistance, which comes from both the right and the left of the political spectrum, more often stems from philosophical, ideological, and emotional sources.

Opposition from the right

On the right, perhaps some of the most vocal opposition comes under the heading of "affordable energy". The American Petroleum Institute and others that follow its line argue that cheap energy helps the economy through faster growth and more exports. Well, in a way, that is true, if we accept a national income accounting system that does not adjust GDP growth downward for the damage done by pollution, and if we don't care whether the goods we export, taking the burden of pollution into account, cost more than we get by selling them.

On the whole, though, international experience provides scant support for the idea that countries with cheap energy prosper while those with expensive energy stagnate. Since crude oil costs about the same everywhere in the world, we can take retail gasoline prices as an indicator of the effect of national energy policy.

Export powerhouses like Germany and South Korea have gasoline prices half again as high as those in the United States. The countries with really cheap gasoline are economic basket cases like Sudan and Venezuela. Why should we be surprised? A market economy works best when prices reflect opportunity costs, externalities included. Economies that fiddle prices to enrich politically-favored producers or consumers are the ones that stagnate.

Abraham Lincoln had a favorite riddle: "How many legs does a dog have, if you call a tail a leg?" Answer: Four. Calling a tail a leg doesn't make it a leg. By the same token, calling underpriced energy "affordable" doesn't make it affordable. Keeping energy prices artificially low just means shifting the true cost to someone else. If there is one thing we really can't afford, it is "affordable energy".

Additional opposition to putting a price on pollution comes from those members of the political right who have a knee-jerk loathing for all taxes. It doesn't matter whether we are talking about emission charges (pollution taxes) or cap-and-trade ("tax-and-trade"). If it walks like a tax, and quacks like a tax, it is a tax and it's a bad idea.

I have some sympathy with that view. The libertarian in me would rather live in a society where social interactions were moderated by market exchange and voluntary mutual assistance, not by tax-financed bureaucracies. However, the realist in me knows that while we are waiting for that utopia to emerge, we have a government and we have to finance it. We can't run it entirely on borrowed funds. If we are going to have a government at all, even if we limit it to providing national defense and enforcing property rights, there is some absolute minimum of tax revenue needed to avoid national bankruptcy – 10 percent of GDP, 20 percent, 25 percent, pick whatever number you like.

Once you pick a number greater than zero for needed tax revenue, then you have to ask which specific taxes are the least bad among all the bad alternatives. A very strong case can be made that revenues from emission charges or from auctioning pollution permits are better than a lot of the alternatives. Rather than distorting the prices of goods and services, emission charges and emission permit revenue, properly calibrated, raise prices by enough to account for environmental spillover effects, thus moving prices toward opportunity costs. Even if you think total taxes are already high enough, you should be willing to embrace pay-for-pollution revenue in order to reduce, dollar-for-dollar, whatever kind of tax you hate even worse – individual income taxes, corporate taxes, payroll taxes, whatever. Hold your nose, and then raise your other hand to vote "Yes" for pollution taxes.

One final source of opposition to pay-for-pollution comes from those on the right who don't think pollution is a problem at all. The most prominent of these are the climate-change deniers. I have attached a lengthy essay on climate change, originally published in the *Cato Journal*, as an appendix to this book. It includes a discussion of issues raised by climate change skeptics. Read it if you want more detail.

Opposition from the left

You might think that if the political right is opposed to paying for pollution, the political left would love the idea, but that is not the case. The progressive left, by and large, is no less opposed than the conservative right, although for rather different reasons.

One reason many liberals and progressives do not embrace paying for pollution is that they really don't believe in the price system at all. They simply do not think that raising the price of gasoline or pesticides or whatever will have any effect on demand. They think that people will go right on polluting however much they please, unless they are stopped from doing so by an absolute government prohibition.

In fact, there is plenty of evidence out there that prices do matter. When gasoline prices go up, people really do cut back their driving. When heating-fuel prices go up, they really do insulate their houses better. When power plants have to pay big bucks to buy marketable permits for all the SO_2 they send up their smokestacks, they suddenly find it profitable to install stack scrubbers or buy low-sulfur coal.

Furthermore, progressive friends of the earth should take into account the fact that putting a price on pollution is by far the best way to affect the behavior of people who are neither environmental activists nor environmental skeptics, but are simply indifferent. It is all well and good to try to raise people's environmental consciousness by holding Earth Day celebrations or handing out reusable shopping bags. Realistically, though, there are a lot of people who brush off all exhortations, or promise to change but then backslide. Raising the price of gas at the pump is going to have a lot bigger impact on the lifestyles of the environmentally indifferent than any number of polar bear calendars.

Beyond the fear that price incentives don't really work, there is a second reason that some progressives prefer command-and-control regulation to market-based incentives. That is their faith in the honesty, competence, and good will of government employees.

In one sense, they are right to have that faith. The federal bureaucracy really is full of honest, competent, hard-working people. At least that is my own experience from the time I spent as a federal bureaucrat during the successful Carter-Reagan drive for transportation deregulation. I went to Washington straight from academia, taking all the usual prejudices with me, but I was pleasantly surprised by the skills and dedication of the people I worked with in government. There was some dead wood, to be sure, but less than in your average university economics department.

However, the honesty and competence of individuals do not guarantee that the bureaucratic institutions they work for will always make good decisions. For one thing, the agencies are all subject to political pressures from assorted special interests, a subject we will return to at length in the next chapter. More importantly, they are also subject to what economists call the *knowledge problem* – the problem that all the knowledge needed to make a decision cannot be assembled in one place.

Let's suppose, for the sake of discussion, that EPA staff can correctly calculate the optimal level of SO_2 emissions for the United States, or at least make as good a guess as anyone else. That is not the end of the problem of regulatory design, only the beginning. In order to implement the target SO_2 level efficiently, regulators would have to know how to allocate cut-backs among thousands of individual pollution sources. Ideally, that should be done while keeping the equimarginal principle in mind. Pollution sources where it is cheaper to achieve an extra ton of abatement should cut back more; those with high marginal abatement costs should cut back less.

How, though, can regulators know where the cutbacks should take place? If they rely on command-and-control methods, they can't. All they can do is mandate equal cutbacks, or a standard pollution-abatement technology, or make some other crude approximation. Because the pattern of abatement is implemented without full knowledge, the cost of achieving the target pollution level is higher than it needs to be. That fact, in turn, hardens industry resistance to the next round of regulation.

The best solution to the impossibility of centralizing knowledge is to tap into the decentralized knowledge, including hands-on tacit knowledge, possessed on-site at all the many pollution sources. That can be done by putting a price on pollution using effective tort law, a cap-and-trade policy, or emission charges, and then letting the polluters sort out their marginal costs for themselves. Given the right incentives, even pollution sources that are not able to articulate their costs explicitly will find out, through trial and error and the use of situational knowhow, by what means they can best reduce pollution.

The bottom line? Paying for pollution is a good idea. It is good for the planet. It is efficient. Since it is impossible to live without having an impact on the environment, it is only fair people should pay for the resources they use and environmental harm they cause, whether their impact is large or small. But putting a price on pollution is not a panacea.

One reason it is not, a reason sometimes neglected by economists who get too wound up in their models, is that not everyone responds rationally to economic incentives. To take a specific example, *The New York Times* recently carried a story about a campaign for better home insulation in the UK[16]. Energy prices there are already among the highest in the world, so the economic incentive to upgrade home insulation is high. Data cited in the article suggest that even with no subsidies, £1,000 invested in a home insulation upgrade would pay for itself in 30 months. That is almost a 40 percent annual rate of return, far higher than the return on any alternative investment available to homeowners. Nonetheless, many people were ignoring this powerful market incentive, and were leaving their homes uninsulated. They were persuaded to join the insulation program only by additional subsidies equal to 40 to 60 percent of the cost of insulation, backed by a vigorous, door-to-door public relations program.

In short, full-cost pricing is necessary, but not always sufficient for achieving environmentally appropriate outcomes. Some people seem to need a nudge, and sometimes even a kick in the pants, before they wake up and see where their own self-interest lies. Often not-for-profit environmental organizations are best positioned to give that nudge or that kick through their education and public relations efforts. Sometimes government agencies need to get involved, too, in educating the public and explaining the rationale of policies, rather than issuing regulations on a set-it-and-forget-it basis.

Finally, material incentives need to be backed up individual responsibility. It is unlikely that we will ever be able to implement a set of policies that fully embody optimal economic incentives, that fully protect all persons and property, and that fully compensate all victims of environmental harms. Still, it is not acceptable to pollute just because some gap in the law makes it possible to do so with impunity, any more than it is acceptable to shoplift just because the storekeeper's back is turned. We must keep in mind that the TANSTAAFL principle is not just a guideline for policy, but also a moral imperative.

---

[16] Elizabeth Rosenthal, "U.S. is Falling Behind in the Business of 'Green,'" *The New York Times,* June 8, 2011.

Chapter 4

THE POLITICAL ECONOMY OF ECOLOGICAL ACTION

Searching
finance

The Efficiency Paradox

In the last chapter, by application of elementary economic analysis, it was shown that pollution and all other types of economic activities which impose external costs on parties not voluntarily taking part in them are sources of inefficiency in the economy. When such external effects are present the price system fails to guide individuals in seeking satisfaction of their material desires exclusively in ways which benefit others at the same time (or at a minimum, leave others unharmed). In the latter part of the chapter several suggestions were made for restructuring the price system and the system of property rights so as to provide people with incentives for abandoning ecologically destructive modes of production and consumption.

In the course of this discussion the astute reader may have been puzzled by one problem. Why is it, he might ask, that we have to go to the trouble of rigging up some special, artificial system of incentives to control pollution? For isn't it true, by definition, that whenever an inefficiency exists in the economy there must also exist at least one way of reallocating resources which would leave at least one individual better off and no one worse off? And if such an opportunity exists, will it not be immediately taken advantage of by the potential beneficiary or beneficiaries, while all other parties maintain an attitude of benign non-intervention? Won't all problems of pollution, then, except perhaps those resulting from irrational malice and ignorance, eventually be taken care of spontaneously through voluntary negotiation among the parties concerned?

These are very interesting questions indeed. Here is an apparent paradox, which we will refer to as the "efficiency paradox." It cannot easily be resolved within the realm of pure economic theory, where human and non-human economic resources appear only as abstract pawns pushed around on an n-dimensional chessboard by an invisible hand linked to an omniscient brain. We must venture into the flesh-and-blood world of political economy, where every economic decision, every reallocation of resources entails not only a readjustment of material relations among things but at the same time of social relations among men.

This chapter will be devoted to exploring some elementary principles of political economy which can help us explain why it is that when individuals have opportunities for securing pure mutual benefit they are not always observed to take advantage of them.

Who Should Pay for the Cleanup?

Although pure economic theory tries as much as possible to avoid normative considerations – those involving such human values as justice, equity, and fair play, where standards may vary widely from individual to individual – in the real world normative considerations cannot be ignored. They often play a crucial role in the making of resource allocation decisions, and we can take the first step toward resolution of the efficiency paradox by introducing one of these normative questions – who should pay for the cleanup?

Suppose that in a certain small community a chemical processing plant is emitting a strong, evil odor which pervades the entire town. It is always difficult to put a cash value on the damage caused in such a case, but, judging by the amount of money people spend to pamper their nostrils with deodorants, perfumes, aerosols, incense, and flowers, let us conservatively assume that each of the 1,000 residents of this community would think it a bargain to be rid of the nuisance for as little as $10. Suppose further that the cost of scrubbing and filtering equipment at the plant which would entirely suppress the odor is estimated at $6,000. What is to be done?

Clearly, the analysis of Chapter 3 applies, and an opportunity for mutual beneficial action to remove the source of the inefficiency exists. Each citizen of the town could contribute $6 to a general fund, to present the factory owner with a big crate of scrubbing and filtering equipment. Each citizen would thus profit to the extent of $4 (since they would get rid of a $10 nuisance at the bargain price of $6), and the owner would have lost nothing.

From the point of view of pure economic theory this would be an excellent scheme, yet an obvious normative objection would surely arise in practice. Why, it would be said, should the citizens of the town pay any part of the cost of pollution abatement? Isn't the plant owner the one who is at fault? Isn't he the aggressor? Do not justice, equity, and fair play require that he bear the cost of cleaning up his establishment, and perhaps pay retroactive damages to the injured parties as well?

This is a powerful and persuasive line of argument, and it goes a long way toward resolving our paradox; for it says that the path of voluntary mutual accommodation, which always exists as a theoretical possibility in the case of any inefficiency, may sometimes be morally unacceptable. To follow this path would seem to many like bargaining with a mugger who has just clubbed you and stolen your billfold, to give him your watch as well in return for a promise not to hit you a second time.

Yet once the path of mutual accommodation is abandoned, the community is divided into two warring factions, and the pro-pollution faction may win the ensuing political struggle. This is particularly true since the factory owner is not likely to be without allies. If he has to clean up he may pass part of the cost along to his customers in the form of a price increase, so his customers may testify on his behalf before the city council. If less of the product can be sold at the higher price, he may have to lay off some of his workers, and thus his employees may join the pro-pollution faction.

The addition of these allies does not alter the normative analysis of the situation, for if the act of pollution itself is a crime then these allies are nothing but partners in crime. The customers of the firm are in a position analytically identical to the recipient of stolen goods. The producer kept his price low only by forcing the residents adjacent to his establishment involuntarily to subsidize the cost of production, by permitting their lungs and noses to be used as industrial waste disposal units, substituting for the mechanical units which should have been installed at the plant. The customers no more deserve to benefit from this tactic than does the owner himself.

The employees of the chemical plant are in no better position. When the boss of a crime syndicate is captured and jailed, do we care for the scores of his henchmen, flunkies, and bodyguards who are forced to seek alternative employment?

It should be mentioned as a theoretical possibility that if every single one of the members of our hypothetical community benefited from the chemical plant as either customer or employee, then the way might be reopened to seek a solution through voluntary mutual accommodation. Except in this extreme case it is certain that those who bear the costs of pollution without receiving any of the benefits of production will object to making any contribution to pollution abatement, saying that no one, owner, shareholder, customer, worker, or city councilman has a right to make his living at the expense of innocent bystanders.

As a final note it should be emphasized that our analysis provides no reason why the consumers of a product, the price of which has been kept artificially low by passing on part of its cost to pollution victims, should not bear at least part of the cost of pollution abatement. Although this seems self-evident the opposition opinion is occasionally voiced. I have heard people complain that if strict automobile emission standards were imposed, the giant corporations which manufacture our cars would be able to pass the cost of installing the necessary emission control devices on to their customers by raising prices. This not only would but should happen. Disposing of waste products is just as much a part of the cost of operating a car as buying gasoline and tires, and in the natural course of things we should expect it to be borne by the car owner.

Some Problems of Organizing Collective Action

The pollution abatement suggestions of Chapter 3 all promoted individual action for improving the habitability of our environment. The incentives provided would help harmonize economic decisions taken by producers and consumers acting independently, thus promoting economic efficiency and ecological rationality. Some other proposals for pollution abatement and environmental improvement are based not on the principle of individual but of collective action. Whenever a group of people are faced with a common environmental problem, suggestions will always be heard that the members of the group should in some way cooperate in pursuing their common interest. In many, if not all cases, even programs like those of Chapter 3, which depend on the principle of individual action for their ongoing operation, may require some sort of collective action to put them into effect in the first place, for example, passing new legislation or repealing old. The problems of organizing individuals to act collectively are of particular interest to the ecological economist, as we will see.

As our situational paradigm let us choose a community suffering from objectionable fumes emanating from fires in an abandoned mine on the edge of town, dug years ago by a company long since bankrupt and out of existence. (Situations much like this exist in many of the old coal mining districts of this country.) Clearly, in contrast to the conditions of our previous example, the possibility of imposing the cost of pollution abatement on those parties which caused the trouble in the first place simply does not exist. Assume a total cleanup bill of $6,000 and a total damage, at $10 per head, of $10,000.

In principle, it would be a good idea to put out the fires and seal off the mine shafts. However, some form of collective action is plainly required to accomplish this, since no individual, acting on his own, is going to put up the whole $6,000 to reap $10 worth of benefits. Not only would it be unprofitable for any individual to undertake the entire project for his own benefit but also it would seem very difficult for a group of citizens to band together and form a corporation to undertake the project as a commercial venture (as might happen if the community needed, say, a new water supply). Because it would not be possible to exclude any member of the community from the benefits of the project once it were carried out, there would be no way to sell the benefits to individuals; all would receive the "product" whether they paid or not.

The mine cleanup project proposed is what economists call a *public good*. Because separate individuals cannot be excluded from enjoying the benefits if they are produced for anyone at all, and because the cost is large relative to the benefits accruing to anyone individual, it is generally held that such goods cannot be supplied by individual action within the framework of the market but must be provided, if at all, by some type of collective action.

Organizing a group of people to supply a public good is a task fraught with pitfalls. Every effort to secure the cooperation of individuals in working together for the common good stumbles against the famous free rider problem. Although every individual would benefit if he, together with all the others, acted cooperatively to secure the public good, he would benefit still more if everyone else worked together to provide the good in question, while he secured the benefit of their effort (from which he cannot, *ex hypothesi*, be excluded) and acted as a free rider. This "let George do it" attitude, which seems to be deeply engrained in human nature, causes no end of difficulty whenever an attempt is made to organize collective action; for if everyone tries to act as a free rider at once, obviously nothing will be accomplished.

It should be noted that the free rider problem occurs in a somewhat wider variety of situations than that suggested by the mine-sealing example. It is likely to be present when efforts are made to organize collective action for preventing the production of a "public bad." It reduces the hopes, for example, of securing the voluntary agreement of all auto owners to install catalytic mufflers, of all campers to abstain from littering, of all beer drinkers to use returnable bottles or urge recycling, of all housewives to use low-phosphate detergents, or of all manufacturers to eliminate excess packaging, even though each of these agreements, were they to come about, might result in clear mutual benefits for all participants. But for this one stumbling block we might ultimately see the adoption of the "new ecological ethic" proposed as a solution to the environmental crisis by ecological evangelists.

The free rider problem is rooted in the tendency of the individual member of a group, when faced with the choice of whether or not to act in the general interest, to assume that the actions of others will not change regardless of his own decision. Suppose, for instance, that we have a lake which is polluted by raw sewage dumped into it from vacation cottages along its shores. If all property owners stopped polluting the lake the increase in its recreational value might compensate them far more than the expense of installing sewage treatment facilities. However, the question which each individual owner will put to himself is, "If all others continue to act as they are acting now, what should I do?" Weighing the considerable expense of treating his own sewage against the negligible benefit of reducing the pollution level of the lake by one one-hundredth or one-thousandth part, he will doubtless continue to pollute. If, by some yet unspecified means, everyone agreed to stop polluting, the same line of reasoning on the part of each individual would soon lead to a breakdown of the agreement. Each would reason that as long as the others continue to treat their sewage, the water will remain adequately clean even if he were to dump his own small contribution of raw effluent.

The analysis of the previous paragraph suggests that the free rider problem might be overcome by changing the characteristics of the situation for the individual in one of two ways. First, things can sometimes be arranged so that it will be worthwhile for the individual to act in the group interest even if others do not follow his example. Second, it is sometimes possible to rig the situation in such a way that it will not be reasonable for the individual to assume that the behavior of others will continue uninfluenced by his own decision. Let us consider each of these possibilities.

The first possible escape from the free rider problem may arise spontaneously if the group in question is sufficiently small. Suppose that the polluted body of water we are considering is a very small pond on which there are only two cottages. In this situation it may well be that each cottage owner will consider the benefit of reducing total pond pollution by 50 percent to be sufficient to justify the expense of installing his own sewage treatment equipment, even if his neighbor does not do likewise. While it is not certain that exactly the optimal amount of sewage treatment equipment will be installed under these circumstances, at least it is likely that some steps will be taken in the right direction.

Generally speaking, the larger the group, the less likely it is that individuals will see it to their own advantage to act in the common interest. However, some techniques have been suggested to extend the applicability of this principle to larger groups. One is to form an organization which simultaneously acts to pursue the common interests of the group and to provide separate benefits to individual members. An example of such an organization in the environmental field is the Sierra Club. This organization carries out activities, such as lobbying for the expansion of National Parks, which are in the common interest of all conservationists. If this were all the organization did, however, it would be difficult to hold together, for non-member, free-riding conservationists would benefit as much as members, and not have to contribute time or money to the work of the club. To hold on to its membership, the organization provides other services as well, such as distributing publications, organizing outings, and so on for its members only. It thus pays the individual to join, if only to secure these private benefits not available to the free rider, and in doing so, he promotes the common interest of the group as well.

The alternative method of avoiding the free rider problem, that of convincing the individual group member that others' actions are not independent of his own, may also arise naturally in sufficiently small groups. Suppose that in either the lake pollution or the mine sealing examples, the total number of individuals involved were large enough so that no one would undertake to defend the common interest on his own, yet small enough so that all were acquainted and came into frequent contact. Suppose further that an informal agreement were made to share the expense of the cleanup among members of the group. It is much more likely that this agreement would be respected than if the group were larger, for now the individual participant will no longer be able to assume that no one would notice if he dropped out to become a free rider. Each party to the agreement will very likely fear that if he sets a bad example by failing to fulfill his share of the mutual obligation, others will follow his lead and the group will soon be back to the less preferable initial situation.

Occasionally this method of circumventing the free rider problem may also be extended to larger groups. One way to do this is somehow to formalize the understanding that continued participation of others will depend on the continued participation of oneself. If our lake had one hundred cottages along its shores a petition might be circulated under the terms of which each signer would pledge to desist from polluting, but only on the condition that at least fifty others agreed to do the same. Assuming that the pledge could be made legally binding, a property owner would be more willing to sign it than to undertake individual action, for in case the quota were not met he would lose nothing at all, and if it were met, he would reap exactly the same benefit as was derived in the earlier example where there were only two cottages on the lake. It is entirely possible that 100 percent of the residents might be willing to sign this conditional pledge, even though none of them would sign an unconditional one to clean up regardless of what others did. This approach could also be successful in raising money to finance a public good, such as the mine-sealing project.

Democracy and Collective Economic Action

In the previous two sections we discovered that even when there are clear mutual gains to be had from agreeing to carry out collectively a program of environmental amelioration, some very sticky normative and organizational problems may make it difficult or impossible to achieve the necessary degree of cooperation by voluntary means. With the prospects for voluntary collective action so limited and uncertain, it is small wonder that one often hears proposals to slice the Gordian knot by dropping the requirement that such action must be organized voluntarily. Wouldn't it be much more straightforward and effective in situations like those of our examples simply to coerce everyone into joining a non-voluntary organization to serve the common interest? Since such proposals are so frequently met with and so frequently put into effect, we must devote a little space to exploring the merits of non-voluntary collective action as a means of achieving our common interest in rational and efficient use of the environment.

In discussing non-voluntary collective action we will limit ourselves to cases where the government provides the framework for organizing the action, and to those possible forms of governmental organizations in which government decisions are made by democratic vote of the citizens of the community in question. We will consider first whether decision making on the basis of democratic voting, with the minority bound to the decisions of the majority, provides a means for attaining economic efficiency in the face of environmental problems, and second whether majority rule conforms with the normative standard suggested earlier, that individuals should not be able to force part of the costs of their own production or consumption activities on to others via the imposition of external effects or other means.

If we begin by analyzing the effects of majority rule in the very simple situations of our earlier examples it appears to be a very attractive approach to environmental decision making. Let us look first at the community which was suffering from the fumes of the abandoned mine. It is clear that if a proposal were put to a referendum to raise $6,000 for the project by a tax levied uniformly on the 1,000 citizens of the town, it would have no difficulty getting a majority of the votes. Since each individual would face the identical possibility of gaining a $10 share of the benefits in return for bearing a $6 share of the costs, it is very likely that the proposal could be approved unanimously. Neither approval nor implementation of the project would be hampered by the free rider problem, since free ridership could now occur only in the form of legally punishable tax evasion.

It is equally likely that the problem of lake pollution could be solved by proposing a measure for referendum which would directly prohibit dumping raw sewage into the water. Again, each property owner would see that his share of the benefits would exceed his share of the costs, and that no free riders would be permitted.

The obvious equity and efficiency of the majority rule principle as applied in these examples naturally raises the hope that it may offer a way out of our troubles in a very wide variety of situations. Unfortunately, these hopes turn out to be largely unfounded, for the smooth functioning of the democratic decision-making process in these examples is a result of two special features and is not generally characteristic of the problems encountered in the real world. One of these features is that the benefits of the proposed project accrue in exactly equal proportion to each member of the community in our examples. The other is that we have considered the projects as if they called for all-or-nothing decisions, without the possibility of intermediate measures.

Suppose that we remove these special features from one of our examples and see what happens. In the mining town let us imagine that the opening from which the fumes emanate is not on the edge of town but within the city limits. Four hundred citizens live to the west of this opening, and the remaining six hundred to the east. The wind blows from the west twice as often as from the east, so that the damage suffered by the western residents is only $5 apiece, while the damage suffered by easterners remains $10 apiece as before. To further alter the situation, let us assume that existing technology allows not only for all-or-nothing control of the fumes but also for any partial degree of control which may be desired. As is the case in a great many economic undertakings, we will imagine that fume control at this mine is subject to some such scale of increasing marginal cost as that shown in Table 4.1. To reduce the emissions by 1 percent may at first be very inexpensive, but further 1 percent reductions become increasingly costly.

Suppose that all 1,000 citizens of this community gather together in a town meeting to listen to fume control proposals and vote on them. At first someone might make the modest proposal that emissions be reduced by 1 percent. The city engineer, called upon to speak, might inform the assembled citizens that the cost of this proposal would be $1. Each easterner, perceiving that he would reap a benefit worth 10¢ to him from a 1 percent reduction in fumes and that his share of the tax burden to support this project would be only 1/10¢, would decide to vote for the project. The westerners would also approve of a 1 percent reduction, getting a 5¢ benefit for 1/10¢ in taxes.

Before this motion were even brought to a vote, an amendment could be offered to increase the degree of control to 2 percent. Consulting the table we can see that this would increase the total cost by $1 more, and again both easterners and westerners would approve.

Table 4.1: Hypothetical cost schedule for fume reduction

Percent reduction	Total cost *(in dollars)*	Marginal cost *(in dollars)*
1	1	
		1
2	2	
		3
3	5	
		5
4	10	
		7
5	17	
		9
...	...	
24	530	
		47
25	577	
		49
26	626	
		51
27	677	
...	...	
49	2305	
		97
50	2402	
		99
51	2501	
		101
52	2602	
...	...	
99	9605	
		197
100	9802	

Continuing in this fashion, the meeting might unanimously approve fume control up to 26 percent. However, with the next proposal, to raise the control level from 26 to 27 percent, the atmosphere of the meeting would suddenly change. From our table, we see that the marginal cost has now risen to $51. This would be fine for the easterners, who would each gain an additional 10¢ benefit at the expense of a 5.1¢ increment in taxes, but what about the westerners? Their 5¢ marginal benefit from this measure is now below the marginal cost to them of sharing the additional expense, so they would vote against it! When the proposal comes to a vote, the tally turns out to be 600 in favor, 400 opposed, and the meeting progresses to the next proposal, to move from 27 to 28 percent.

The next change in the voting occurs when the 51 percent control level is reached. When the suggestion is made to move on to 52 percent it is discovered that the additional tax burden per citizen of 10.1¢ is greater than the benefit even to the easterners. This next proposal, then, will not get a single vote, and the meeting will adjourn, having reached a final decision to reduce fume emission from the abandoned mine by a total of 51 percent.

Although the town meeting just described may perfectly exemplify participatory democracy, government by consent of the governed, majority rule, and many other sacred and glorious American political principles, its performance must nonetheless be rated as very poor by the standards which we have been employing. The same normative objection applies to the decision reached by the meeting as was discussed in the second section of this chapter. Some individuals (the easterners) are enjoying the benefits, part of the cost of which is imposed on others (the westerners) against their will, just as in our previous example, the polluting producer imposed part of his cost on the residents near his factory. The only difference lies in the mechanism by which the costs are involuntarily imposed on the non-beneficiaries. In the one case, the costs were transferred by means of pollution, and in the other, by means of taxation.

Normative objections aside, the 51 percent cleanup decision reached by the town meeting is not even efficient. The origin of the inefficiency is easy to see. Each citizen, in deciding whether or not to vote for an increase in pollution control, weighed marginal benefits received against marginal costs imposed. Applying the equimarginal principle, the westerners would have liked only a 26 percent abatement program, while the easterners, applying the same reasoning, opted for 51 percent. Thus, under the system of majority rule governing the meeting, it was inevitable that the majority coalition of easterners, each applying the equimarginal principle to maximize his own net advantage, would force the westerners involuntarily to violate that same principle!

Looking at the matter another way, we can easily apply our standard efficiency test to the 51 percent decision, by seeing if its implementation would still leave room for a further mutually beneficial agreement among the townspeople. Such potential agreement does indeed turn out to exist. Simply consider the effect of cutting back pollution control from 51 to 50 percent. The easterners would each lose 10¢ in benefits, partially compensated for by a reduction of 9.9¢ in taxes, for a net loss of 0.1¢ each, or a grand total of 60¢ for the whole group. Each westerner, on the other hand, would lose a 5¢ benefit, but would be more than compensated by the 9.9¢ tax reduction, ending up with a net gain of 4.9¢, or a total of $19.60 for all westerners combined. Clearly, all parties would gain if the westerners banded together and offered a collective cash payment of somewhere between $.60 and $19.60 to the easterners, in return for a cutback to 50 percent pollution control. A series of such deals could in principle be negotiated until the degree of pollution control had been cut to 41 percent. (The reader might wish to verify as an exercise that at this point, where total marginal costs to all parties just equal total marginal benefits, an efficient degree of pollution control is reached, and that no further mutually beneficial agreements are possible.)

It is relatively unlikely that the series of deals just described could actually be carried out in practice, since any attempt to carry them out would encounter all of the by now familiar normative and organizational difficulties characteristic of voluntary collective action. It would be much more likely that the inequitable and inefficient 51 percent decision would be the one actually put into effect.

This somewhat lengthy example of the town meeting illustrates a very important general principle – that democratic voting is not an efficient method of making resource allocation decisions. This principle applies with particular force to decisions concerning public projects which confer special, differential benefits on a portion of the population and which are financed out of taxes levied on beneficiaries and non-beneficiaries alike.

In our example the misallocation of resources was in the direction of overfunding the project. Although the voting process might, in theory, also result in underfunding (suppose that in our example the westerners had been in the majority), there is reason to believe that in a complex representative democracy, like that of the United States, overfunding of public projects is more likely to be the case. Overfunding occurs when those parties receiving the largest benefits exert the strongest influence in the decision of the level at which the project is to be carried out. At least three factors favor the occurrence of this situation even when the beneficiaries may be numerically a minority of the population. First, since benefits are very often concentrated and highly prominent, while the costs of anyone project are widely diffused and thus barely noticeable to the individual taxpayer, legislative representatives are apt to discover that voters pay more attention to the visible benefits than the invisible costs when deciding which way to vote in the next election. Second, a group of potential beneficiaries, if few in number and especially if already belonging to an ongoing interest-related organization, may easily be able to act collectively in lobbying for a given project, while the multitude of non-beneficiaries, for all the reasons discussed above, may not be able to act together to thwart it. Finally, various types of legislative vote-trading – particularly those known as logrolling and porkbarreling – often make it possible to tie together several special-interest projects into a package deal acceptable to a majority of legislators.

For these reasons the legislative output of a representative government typically takes the form of a large number of special programs, each one of which benefits one minority group at the expense of the general public, and each one of which, taken separately, is overfunded. This fact is of profound importance for ecological economics, for it means that democratically-organized collective action for improvement of the environment may be liable to precisely the same normative and economic objections as are the acts of pollution and environmental destruction which they are meant to counteract, namely, 1. that the result of such action is to confer benefits on some at the expense of costs borne involuntarily by others and 2. that as a result of such action scarce economic and environmental resources are subject to inefficient and wasteful misallocation!

Is there no way in which we as citizens can act together, within the framework of our institutions of government, to cope with the environmental crisis? Fortunately, one type of governmental action is free from these objections-if that action is the adoption of a measure which corrects a situation in which some individual or individuals previously forced part of the costs of production or consumption off on others by means of environmental externalities. If the offenders are made to pay the full costs themselves, the result is not to institute a new inefficiency but to remove an old one, and not to initiate a fresh inequity but to terminate one which has unjustly been permitted to exist in the past. The reader will find that all of the recommendations for the enactment or repeal of legislation at the federal, state, or local level which I recommend in this book fall into this category.

Unfortunately, the likelihood of existing institutions of democratic government adopting measures of this type and limiting themselves to these alone is rather small. We have seen that even the direct, participatory democracy of a town meeting can go astray in the field of environmental legislation. In the tangled jumble of representative bodies, administrative agencies, and regulatory commissions, where democracy fitfully struggles to function in the real world, the outlook is bleaker still. The opportunities for logrolling, porkbarreling, lobbying, favoritism, and corruption are sufficiently great that the political process all too often responds to the wishes of those who would destroy the environment at the expense of those who would benefit by its preservation, and all too often guards special interests and privileges more vigilantly than the general interest in maintaining economic efficiency and ecological rationality.

Yet to say that realism counsels pessimism provides no excuse for hiding one's head in the sand. A public aware of the basic principles of economics and ecology will surely see their environment degraded at a less rapid rate than if they were easy marks for duplicity and manipulation. It is with this modest educational aim in mind that this volume has been written.

Commentary

What has changed

Public choice economics is based on the premise that asking what governments should do is not enough. We also need to ask what they do in reality. Public choice economists seek answers to questions about the actual behavior of governments by looking at the rational self-interest of elected officials, bureaucrats, and ordinary voters. The field, which was in its infancy in 1971, has now matured into a mainstream branch of the economics profession.

Public choice theory is applicable as much to environmental policy as to any other area. A survey of the literature on the political economy of environmental policy in the 2003 *Handbook of Environmental Economics* cites nearly a hundred books and articles, and many more have been published since that time[17]. One case study after another has confirmed that special interests are able to use mechanisms such as lobbying, campaign contributions, and logrolling to exert disproportionate influence. Policies that result in less than the optimal degree of environmental protection, or that achieve a given level of protection at an unnecessarily high cost, are all too often the outcome.

Another strand of the public choice literature has linked environmental regulation to the theory of regulatory capture that originated with the work of George Stigler, Sam Pelzman, and others in the 1970s. According to that theory, regulations are best viewed not as constraints placed on industry by government, but as services provided by government to industry. Environmental regulations can be manipulated to raise barriers to entry and enforce cartel-like cooperation in place of competition. For example, laws controlling acid rain place greater restrictions on emissions from newly built factories and power plants than from existing ones. These "grandfather" provisions make it harder for new competitors to enter the market.

---

17 *Handbook of Environmental Economics*, Jeffrey Vincent and Karl-Goran Maler, eds, North-Holland, 2003.

What has not changed

As a whole, public choice economics supports the idea that environmental policy should rely as much as possible on market mechanisms. However, it also provides grounds for caution, in that even the most market-oriented policy initiatives can emerge in distorted form when subjected to the pressures of real world politics. The failure in 2010 of the American Clean Energy and Security Act (ACES, also known as Waxman-Markey) provides a case in point.

Economists are nearly unanimous in agreeing that pollution control policy should, whenever possible, use the price system to force polluters to pay for the harm they do. There is less agreement as to whether the tort-law approach, pollution taxes, or cap-and-trade is the best way to implement full-cost pricing. Libertarian purists tend to favor the tort-law approach because it defends property rights directly through the court system, without depending on a regulatory bureaucracy. Economists who focus on reaching an optimal level of pollution in the most efficient manner tend to favor pollution taxes. Still others favor a cap-and-trade approach on the grounds that it is more feasible from a public choice point of view, despite having some technical drawbacks compared to a tax.

The public choice argument for cap-and-trade is based on the idea that control over the initial allocation of pollution permits gives lawmakers a tool for building a winning political coalition. A successful strategy could have several components.

One component could be sale of at least some permits at auction. The revenue thus raised could either be rebated to the public to offset the distributional effects of the program or directed to specific projects such as research or job training in order to win the support of important constituencies. Revenues from auctioning permits could even be used to reduce the general government deficit if there is a constituency that favors doing so.

Alternatively, some or all permits could be given away free of charge to buy the support of key players. For example, distributing permits on a "grandfather" basis could bring about a political split among existing sources, who might otherwise unanimously oppose pollution control. Polluters who get free permits and have lower-than-average abatement costs would find that they could make a profit by reducing their own emissions and selling their permits on the open market. That would bring them on board the pro-control coalition. Only those sources who had higher-than-average abatement costs, and who would thus end up as permit buyers, would remain in opposition.

Finally, some have hoped that the "cap-and-trade" label would make paying for pollution politically palatable to die-hard opponents of any and every form of taxation. Although the impact of the scheme on polluters who ended up having to buy permits would not be much different from that of a pollution tax, it avoids open use of the dreaded "T-word."

All this sounds like clever political strategy. Unfortunately, in the case of Waxman-Markey, the coalition-building power of cap-and-trade turned out to be less than some had hoped. In order to assemble a winning coalition in the House of Representatives, not just a few, but nearly all permits were handed out for free. (In contrast, candidate Obama's 2008 campaign platform on cap-and-trade had called for all permits to be auctioned.) Worse than that, a large block of permits was squandered on a scheme that would have prevented utilities from passing pollution-control costs along to consumers. That provision would have undermined one of the biggest potential incentives for energy conservation. Finally, beyond its basic cap-and-trade mechanism, the Waxman-Markey bill was loaded with a grab-bag of command-and-control provisions, including renewable energy mandates, research subsidies, and appliance efficiency standards. What remained was a muddled piece of legislation that departed widely from the market-based efficiency of a simple cap-and-trade plan.

The Waxman-Markey bill did pass the House of Representatives, but when the debate moved over to the Senate, the coalition behind it collapsed entirely. So much had been given away to win a House majority that there was little room left for further vote-buying and logrolling. When the Republican leadership decided to re-brand cap-and-trade as "cap-and-tax", the few remaining Republican supporters dropped away. By the time the bill finally died, it was so far from what it had started out to be that few tears were shed by supporters of rational environmental policy.

In short, advances in the theory of public choice may have given us new insights into the process of policy making, but they have not led to dependable improvements in policy outcomes.

Chapter 5

COPING WITH THE POPULATION EXPLOSION

Searching
finance

What Are We in For?

There is an old story about a very wise man who invented a new game for the edification and amusement of his emperor – chess. The emperor was so delighted with the new pastime that he told the inventor to name his own reward, and he would receive it. "Sire," the man said, "I am a humble man of modest needs, and I ask only this: that you give me a single grain of wheat for the first square on the chessboard, two grains for the second square, four for the third, then eight, and so on until you have worked your way to the last square on the board."

The emperor at first insisted that the inventor take more than this, perhaps a bushel of gold coins or the pick of his harem, but when the man stuck to his original request the order was given for a servant to bring a jar of grain from the kitchen, and the counting began.

A single grain was placed on the first square, two on the second, then four, eight, sixteen, thirty-two ... until, lo and behold, when the emperor reached the fourteenth square, counting out 8,192 grains, the jar which had been brought from the kitchen was emptied! A second jar was brought, but it sufficed only for the fifteenth square. Stubbornly, the emperor demanded that his kitchen be emptied, and all of his storehouse was wheeled in on a huge cart loaded with a thousand jars of wheat. Yet when the 8,388,608 grains required for the twenty-fourth square had been counted out, this cart too was emptied. At this point, the ruler, seeing what he was in for, called for the captain of his guard and gave the order that the wise inventor of the game of chess should be quietly garroted.[18]

This fable, like all such fables, has a moral: Playing around with runaway geometric progressions will get you in trouble sooner or later.

Let us see how this moral applies to the growth patterns of animate populations. Suppose we take a single yeast cell and place

---

[18] And well he did so! To cover the board in the fashion suggested would have required no fewer than $18,446,744,073,709,551,615$ grains of wheat, about a billion tons.

it on a culture dish (or take a pair of fruit flies and put them in a small cage, or a pair of dogs and put them on an island previously inhabited only by rabbits). Then, let us watch and see what happens to the population of the organism as time goes by.

At first the population will grow in simple geometric progression, like the grains on the chessboard. The biological characteristics of the species will determine some normal, fixed doubling time under optimal conditions, and the population will follow a path approximately like curve A in Figure 5.1.

Sooner or later, though, the population will begin to fill up its bottle or island or whatever, and the time needed to double the population in the more crowded conditions will increase. With fixed environmental limits the population curve will follow an S-shape like curve B in our figure. The deteriorating conditions for reproduction and survival as the population ceiling is approached eventually bring population growth to a complete halt.

Figure 5.1 Hypothetical population growth curves

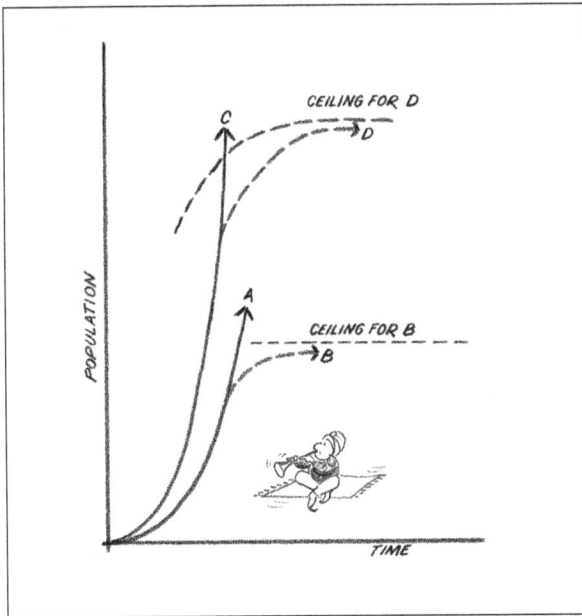

Does this simple S-curve law of population growth apply to human populations as well? In the long run it surely does. In the short run, however – let us say over the period of the last two centuries – the curve of human population growth has departed from the normal S-shape because of man's ability to alter his environment in certain ways which a fruit fly or yeast cell cannot do. In particular, principally because of advances in medical science, the human population has not been subjected to a fixed doubling time but to a steadily shortening one. The world population is now doubling about once every thirty-five years. The last doubling took about eighty years, the one before that some two hundred, and earlier ones longer still. To put it another way, not only has the human population grown but the rate of its growth has grown also.

No less significantly, advances in agricultural and industrial technology have effectively increased the size of the globe over the last two centuries, in terms of the maximum population which it will support.

Taken together, these two factors have so far kept the curve of human population growth from reaching the point where it would bend over to make an S-shape. What will the future bring? Some optimistic souls think that the curve will just keep going right on up like curve C in the figure. It has been estimated that the earth alone could accommodate twenty million times its present population, living at 120 per square meter in a 2,000-story building covering the entire earth. It would take us 890 years, at our present rate of growth, to get to that point, and by then we may have solved the formidable technical and economic problems of interstellar travel, and be able to export our surplus to the stars (assuming the natives will supply us with the requisite number of immigrant visas).[19]

If people want to believe in this sort of thing there is no rational argument which can be presented to convince them otherwise. If one were to "prove" that it is impossible to travel faster than the

---

[19] The 2,000-story building, space flight, and many other fascinating topics are discussed in a very worthwhile book compiled by Garrett Hardin: *Population, Evolution, and Birth Control*, 2nd ed. (San Francisco: W. H. Freeman and Company, 1969).

speed of light and reach the stars, they could legitimately counter by citing "proofs" by eminent 19th-century scientists that heavier-than-air machines could never fly. For the present, however, curve C of Figure 5.1 lies in the realm of pure speculation, not of reasoned discussion, so we will give it no further consideration but go on instead to explore the implications of the more interesting alternative for the future of population growth as represented by curve D.

Curve D shows what would happen if we were to exhaust the technological possibilities for further raising the population ceiling. As the ceiling stops rising, and the population curve approaches it, the latter would necessarily bend over and assume the standard S-shape. Eventually, a condition of population equilibrium would be established, in which births just equaled deaths and each generation just reproduced itself.

Simply to say that a finite ceiling to population growth dictates an eventual approach to population equilibrium is not quite enough, for there is more than one way to achieve population equilibrium. The first type of equilibrium, beloved of the classical economists, is what we can call the marginal subsistence solution. Imagine a society for which there is some fixed population ceiling dictated by existing, fixed technology. Suppose that the reproductive behavior of the populace is such that each generation more than reproduces itself, consumer goods are available only via purchase, and income is not distributed equally over all members of society. As population grows, given the fixed technology, it is reasonable to assume that the prices of living space and food will rise relative to wages. Eventually, the poorest classes of society will be so disadvantaged by the rising cost of living that their conditions for reproduction and survival will be adversely affected. (Perhaps their birth rate will fall because of crowding, or their death rate will rise because of disease and malnutrition.) In any event, population growth ceases for these poorest classes, lowering the average for society as a whole. As population grows still more (at its now diminished rate), the next most prosperous group of families is pushed to the subsistence level. At the same time the first group may be expected to fall below the subsistence minimum, that is, to be pushed to such depths of poverty that deaths exceed births among them. The average population growth rate thus drops still further. In this way the margin of subsistence is pushed higher up the income ladder so that eventually excess births among the prosperous are just balanced by excess deaths among the destitute, and equilibrium is achieved.

This marginal subsistence solution to population growth was the "dismal theorem" advanced by T.R. Malthus in his famous book, *An Essay on the Principle of Population*. Its picture of a society in which affluence can exist only against the backdrop of miserable masses whose numbers are continuously replenished by the excess children of the rich driven down into poverty is indeed dismal.

Yet there exists a second type of population equilibrium more dismal still. We can call this the absolute subsistence solution. Suppose that the society which we are considering is the same as before, except that certain essential consumer goods – a minimum of food, clothing, and shelter – are available not solely via purchase but also, for those too poor to buy them, from public stocks purchased through taxation and distributed free of charge. Now, as population grows and prices rise, the lowest economic strata of society, rather than sinking below the subsistence level, simply make greater and greater use of public soup kitchens. As the number of clients of these increases, and as the price of the provender distributed rises, the burden of taxation placed upon the prosperous grows ever larger, accelerating their slide into poverty. All the while population growth continues, until eventually a situation is reached when everyone is patronizing the soup kitchens. At this point the opportunities for taxation are obviously exhausted, so the relief recipients themselves must go to work to produce their own rations. Eventually, when these rations are barely sufficient to give the strength needed for communal food production, the toilers returning home at the end of the day too tired and hungry to reproduce at a rate higher than the death rate, population equilibrium will be achieved.

Kenneth Boulding has called this line of reasoning the "utterly dismal theorem," for the only result of the charity designed to assuage Malthusian misery is ultimately to increase the sum total of human pain and suffering.

It should be noted that a dynamic variant of both the marginal and absolute subsistence solutions is possible. If we allow for some technological advance, but only enough to raise the population ceiling at a rate less rapid than the growth rate of population implicit in the reproductive behavior of well-fed members of society, a situation occurs in which either the dismal or the utterly dismal configuration is reproduced each year on a somewhat larger scale. Only if the rate of technological progress is sufficient to outrun population will things get better, given the assumptions we have been using. This is exactly what happened in Malthus' England for the next two hundred years or so following the publication of his book. But remember that we can't count on the indefinite continuation of such a rate of technological progress.

Is our only choice between the dismal and the utterly dismal? No, not quite. A third possibility exists, at least in principle, of a non-subsistence solution. Suppose that something happened to bring the birth rate and death rate of a society into equality at a higher-than-subsistence standard of living. There are many ways in which this possibility might come to pass. A fad of celibacy or homosexuality might sweep the nations of the world. The frequency and ferocity of wars might increase. Esthetic and cultural standards might spontaneously become biased against large families. Increased use of herbicides, pesticides, and peaceful atomic energy might bring about an increased incidence of sterility and fatal birth defects. The Pharaoh might send around his troops to slaughter every eldest male child. The possibilities are endless, if not all equally attractive. Is there any chance that one of them might come to pass? We will investigate the prospects for our own country in the remainder of this chapter, and for developing nations in the next.

The Not-So-Simple Arithmetic of Population Growth

Anyone who has read *The Population Bomb*[20] is familiar with the simple arithmetic of population growth. To calculate the rate of population growth in a given country in a given year, you find the Crude Birth Rate (CBR, the number of babies born per 1,000 of population in the given year), subtract from that the Crude Death Rate (CDR, the number of deaths per 1,000 of population in the given year), and divide by ten to express the result as a percentage. For example, in Costa Rica in the late fifties, the CBR was 47.7 per 1,000 and the CDR was 9.6 per 1,000, so that the Rate of Natural Increase of Population (RNI) was 47.7 − 9.6 = 38.1 per 1,000, or 3.81 percent per annum. For the same period in Luxembourg the figures were 15.9 −11.9 = 4.0, or .04 percent per annum.

The next lesson in population arithmetic comes with the translation of population growth rates expressed in percentage terms to population growth rates expressed as doubling times. A population which kept up the rate reported above for Costa Rica over a sustained period would double every 18 years. The doubling time for the population of Luxembourg would be a comfortable 173 years at the 0.4 percent rate. It's a good thing for Luxembourg, too, since the population density there is already a solid 123 per square kilometer!

On the basis of this much population arithmetic, we can have all sorts of fun and games. Remember the chess board? If Costa Rica kept growing at its present rate until the year 2100, its population would increase from its 1961 population of 1,225,000 to 250 million, about the population of the Soviet Union today. These people would be packed in no fewer than 4,800 per square kilometer, compared with a mere 3,000 or so per square kilometer in today's Hong Kong, the present record holder. If the 317,000 people of Luxembourg had been the only inhabitants of the world in the fourth century B.C., and had increased their population at no faster rate than the snail's

---

[20] Paul R. Ehrlich, New York: Ballantine Books, 1968.

pace – 4/10 of 1 percent – which they maintain at present, the world would nonetheless be up to its current population of over 3 billion in 1970.

Population arithmetic like this is downright frightening! And that's just what it's supposed to be. It's supposed to frighten you, to panic you into doing something, now, to stop the population explosion. But, adhering to that old adage of "look before you leap", prior to getting down to recommendations for population policy, let's take a more careful look at the not-so-simple arithmetic of population growth.

Forget about Luxembourg and Costa Rica for awhile, and take a look at population statistics for the United States. Ehrlich gives a doubling time of sixty-three years for the U.S., which translates into a per annum rate of about 1.1 percent. Does this mean that, unless we change our current patterns of reproductive behavior, by the 400th Fourth of July there will be 1.2 billion Americans saluting the flag and tossing beer cans into our lakes and rivers? It means no such thing. The key phrase is "our current patterns of reproductive behavior." What we must do is clarify the question of the relationship between our patterns of -reproductive behavior and the rate of population growth.

We can begin by noticing that the much bandied-about Rate of Natural Increase is determined by a combination of two factors – our patterns of reproductive behavior and mortality *and* the age distribution of the population. If reproductive behavior were to remain unchanged over a great many years eventually a stable relationship between mortality-fertility patterns and the age distribution of the population would emerge, at which point the crude Natural Increase rate would accurately reflect long-term population trends. However, in periods when reproductive behavior has been changing in the recent past the Natural Increase figure may be very misleading. If the propensity to reproduce has fallen in the recent past, as it has in the U.S., the RNI exaggerates prospects for population growth. Why? Because people generally have children when they are young, and die when they are old. The people that are now in the high-mortality brackets are members of the relatively small generation born around the turn of the century, while those in the high fertility range are members of the much larger generation who were their children. If the currently fertile generation is having, on the average, smaller families than their parents did, we may anticipate that by the time they age, the numerical disproportion between generations will be less than at present. This will automatically show up in higher Crude Death Rates, lower Crude Birth Rates, and a lower Rate of Natural Increase even if the average family size of children now being born does not decrease further.

To avoid all this confusion and isolate the true, underlying trend of population growth is a very complex mathematical problem. Without getting too abstruse we can take one more step which may shed some further light on the subject. Avoiding the terminology of birth and death rates altogether, let us restate the conditions for population growth and stability as follows: Take an imaginary group of female infants, all born at the same moment. Follow them all through life until death, being sure to count those who die in infancy. Count the total number of female children born to members of this group in their 1,000 lifespans. Then take the ratio of daughters to mothers. This ratio is called the Net Reproduction Rate (NRR). If the NRR is exactly equal to one, then the population is just replacing itself. If it is less than one, the generation of daughters has fewer members than the generation of mothers and the population will shrink. If the NRR exceeds one, the population will grow.

For the reasons given above, a fall in the NRR does not immediately show up in the rate of natural increase of population; yet it is the NRR which is the crucial figure for long-run population growth. Modern Japan provides a dramatic example. The CBR is 16.6 and the CDR is 6.4, giving an RNI of 1.2 percent per annum. But does Japan face a long-run population problem? Only if too few people are a problem, for the underlying NRR of .92 tells us that after a few more years of growth the Japanese population will, if current patterns prevail, begin a long, steady decline!

What about the U.S? The ponderous tomes in which professional demographers advance their guarded estimates of trends in mortality, fertility, and the Net Reproduction Rate are worth digging through. From what I can gather, perusing this literature strictly as a layman, it appears that the NRR in the U.S. has been falling for some time, is already very close to the magic value of 1.0, and is expected to reach that level and continue to drop below it sometime about 1975.[21]

This does not mean that the rate of population growth will immediately fall to zero in 1975. It may even accelerate slightly for a few years as the children of the postwar baby boom reach their age of maximum fertility. But soon, growth will taper off and finally population will gradually decline.

The likelihood that the NRR will soon fall below 1.0 has some interesting implications for some of the population control schemes advanced for this country. Consider an often mentioned scheme originated by the fertile imagination of Kenneth Boulding.[22] Boulding would require each mother to obtain a special permit or license before giving birth to a child. (Never mind how one would go about enforcing this against someone who showed up at the emergency room in labor without her ticket.) The permits would be distributed as follows: Each child, male and female, would be given one permit, good at any time, when they were born. Each married couple would thus automatically have two such permits. (If a child died in infancy its permit might revert to the parents to give them a second chance.) Any person, married or single, who did not want children could sell his permit to any couple who wanted a family of more than two.

Boulding evidently anticipates that a lively market would develop in these permits, rather like the Stock Exchange, with speculators, Dow – Jones indexes – the works. Many people have

---

21 See, for example, Donald J. Bogue, *Principles of Demography* (New York: John Wiley & Sons, Inc., 1969), pp. 883-893.

22 In *The Meaning of the 20th Century* (New York: Harper & Row, 1964). An excerpt is included in the collection by Hardin, *op. cit*

assumed that the price established for a certificate would be quite high, and have worried about such possibilities as rich whites buying up all the certificates of poor blacks. In fact, no such thing would happen. The price of a baby permit would clearly depend on the Net Reproduction Rate. As soon as the NRR fell to or below unity, as it appears about to do in this country, the price of certificates would automatically fall to zero! Any couple who wanted could have as many children as they pleased, despite the existence of this seemingly Draconian birth control legislation.

In my opinion, formed on the basis of what is currently known about demographic trends in the United States,[23] the best population policy for our government to adopt is no policy at all. Unfortunately, my opinion is not currently being heeded, for our government does now have some legislation on the books in this field. I am referring to the income tax exemption, and certain other government programs for child support, which encourage people to have large families. I can see no more justification for the government to subsidize population growth than to legislate against it. Family subsidies have to go. If the poor are to be given relief of some sort, let their payments be independent of family size. If programs like a guaranteed annual income are going to be instituted, make this income sufficient for a childless couple to live comfortably and a family of four to live decently. Any who would not avail themselves of the opportunities to keep their family size below eight or ten could justly be left either to scrimp and save and stretch their fixed guaranteed annual budget as best they could or to find, on their own initiative, some way of supplementing this budget. Cessation of all current government programs to promote population growth would, I should think, knock the last few points off the NRR even before 1975.

---

[23] Of course, if the unexpected were to happen, and the NRR to reverse its trend and rise abruptly, I might be willing to reopen this discussion.

Is There an Optimal Population Size?

Perhaps some readers are convinced, by the argument advanced in the previous section, that population growth in the United States will one day soon spontaneously grind to a halt, but would still dispute the conclusion that no government population control measures are justified. For how do we know, these readers might say, that the level of population which we arrive at by chance will be the optimal level? Isn't it possible that population growth will stop too soon, leaving us with too few people? Or isn't it possible that population growth has already gone on too long, so that we are already overcrowded? Shouldn't we set some national goal of XYZ millions of persons, and make every effort to arrive at this goal in the shortest possible time?

Let us examine a few of the more frequently heard arguments on this score. A good starting point is the "Chamber of Commerce" argument, that large population size is good for business. If a sufficiently narrow conception of the phrase "good for business" is taken, there is some truth to the contention, for in comparing two communities of different size or a single community at two periods in time, it is generally true that other things being equal the total volume of sales for all businesses will be larger when the community is more populous. But probing a little deeper, certain questions arise as to whether this fact, even if accepted as true, would justify an expansionary population policy. An expansion of the total sales for all businesses would not seem widely beneficial unless it represented at the same time an expansion of sales per capita. Suppose Smithville and Jonesville both start in 1960 with a population of 10,000 and total retail sales of $30 million ($3,000 per capita). By 1970 Smithville doubles its population, and increases sales to $80 million ($4,000 per capita), while Jonesville "stagnates," retaining its population of 10,000 and boosting its total volume of business to a mere $50 million ($5,000 per capita). The Chamber of Commerce of Smithville will no doubt boast loud and long of the superior performance of their town, but where would you rather live? There is little basis in economic theory for the contention that increasing population makes business any better on a per capita basis.

Or is there? What about the more sophisticated variant of the "good for business" argument that says that population growth is necessary to keep us out of a recession? This turns out to be nothing but a rerun of the old "underconsumption" or "secular stagnation" argument. It is true that if a bungling government insisted on getting us into a permanent recession by pursuing deflationary monetary and fiscal policies year after year, a spurt of population growth might provide the spur for business recovery. But wouldn't it be better just to change economic policy? Proper management of fiscal and monetary policy could probably provide us with prosperity and rapid growth of per capita income even in a period of contracting population. Trying to use population control as an instrument of macroeconomic policy is about as enlightened a technique as burning down the barn to roast the pig.

Having dispatched the advocates of population control from the chambers of commerce, we must whirl about to face a new set of attackers, those from the Pentagon. These proponents of an expansionary population policy are bent on striking terror in our hearts with a formidable weapon indeed, a modernized, cyberneticized, cost-effectivized version of the "yellow peril"! As Colin Clark puts it, writing in the *National Review*,[24] "As far as we can see it now, the prospects for fifty years hence are of a world in which both the United States and Soviet Russia have fallen out of the race [for world power status] in a world dominated by the Asian countries, with India and China in the lead, and Pakistan and Indonesia as the runners up." For a moment (no longer), let us assume it is indeed true that the index of human wellbeing by which our government should be guided in its every decision is the maximizaton of military power at all costs. Must we then concede that population equals power? It is far from obvious that we must.

---

[24] May 20, 1969; reprinted in Walt Anderson, ed., *Politics and Environment* (Pacific Palisades, California: Goodyear Publishing Company, 1970)

Making war is like growing grain; you can do it with a lot of people with hoes or a few people with combines. And which is the more effective grain-growing force, the 300-million-man Indian "agricultural army" or the 20-million-man American force? Remember the Second World War? Those Germans put up an excellent fight against the combined forces of all the Allied countries, boasting many times the German population. The Allies won *not* by using a larger number of more poorly equipped troops. Quite the opposite, at first the Germans gained great victories with their initially more sophisticated equipment, and the tide was not turned until the Allies were able to overtake and surpass them in the output of military hardware.

I suspect that the inhabitants of "underpopulated" Sweden and the Netherlands, who lost their world-power status at the end of the 17th century, are laughing up their sleeves at American generals who would like to trade places with their Indian and Chinese counterparts. Come to think of it, if we exported all our generals to China, wouldn't that in itself be a partial solution to our population problem?

Next in line behind the generals as advocates of an activist population policy come assorted politicians and quasipolitical spokesmen. Among these a particularly interesting group of population growth advocates were flushed out by the results of the latest census. Every type of individual, it seems, has one overriding goal in life. For businessmen it is expansion of sales (or profits, if you take the old-fashioned view); for generals, it is augmentation of the kill capacity; and for mayors and governors, it appears to be the maximization of federal grants and subsidies. Now, since many of these federal grants and subsidies are handed out on a per capita basis, one way to get more money for your city is to get more people into it. Never mind if per capita aid remains the same – it is the aggregate total which must grow to give you clout in the halls of Congress, and give you something to boast about at the next mayors' or governors' conference. So we saw the spectacle, when the census results were in, of outraged politicians everywhere crying that there must have been a miscount, that their fiefdom just had to have more inhabitants than the official tabulations showed.

But if the politicians who are in power want to increase the population, what about the politicians who are out of power? Naturally, they want more population too – at least if it is their own minority constituency where the multiplication takes place. This population-equals-power mentality is nowhere more evident than among those black leaders who cry "genocide" whenever education or legislation attempts to help our citizens freely choose the family size they would like. Their reasoning is that black people will, in the long run, be better off if they are more numerous, for then their voting power will increase. The last part is true enough, but will it be the black people or the black politicians who will be better off in this future era of stuffed ballot boxes and empty stomachs? It is interesting to note in passing that the "genocide" line is popular even among those radicals who admit the futility of advancing welfare via the ballot box, for they are interested in a maximum supply of cannon fodder to man the barricades on the day of the revolution. (I would not wish to imply that blacks as an ethnic group have a monopoly on any of the above lines of reasoning.)

All of the special interest groups mentioned so far have had one thing in common: Their idea of the optimal population is larger than the numbers we have at present. The conservationists, in contrast, want a population smaller than the current one. They have their own interests to defend. Just as generals want recruits, and politicians want huddled masses yearning to pay taxes and collect subsidies, conservationists have a burning desire for wide-open spaces and wilderness areas – trampled and crowded by the minimum possible number of fellow backpackers and naturalists. Since nature lovers seem to be born in a certain fixed proportion to the population, and since the prospects for further expansion of wilderness areas are, to say the least, dim, it follows with logical precision that the smaller the population the better off will be those conservationists among them.

But conservationists will say, "You are making a parody of us! We are not like those other special interest groups – the militarists, the politicians, or the greedy Capitalists! We speak for the interests of society as a whole, and have sound, reasoned arguments to back up our position." Fair enough. Let's take a look at these arguments.

A full-page ad in *The New York Times*[25] maintains that the fight against pollution "will be a losing battle unless we check our rapidly growing population, which is an underlying cause of the pollution of our environment." This doctrine, I submit, is at best highly misleading and at worst utterly fallacious. It is simply not true either that population growth necessarily causes increased pollution of the environment or that a halt to population growth would by itself stabilize or decrease the amount of pollution produced by our economy. The two problems of population pressure and pollution abatement are, both conceptually and in practice, quite separate and distinct.

Harking back to what was said on the subject in an earlier chapter, it will be recalled that an act of pollution is a form of trespass on the rights or property of others, an act in which individual A imposes a cost or burden on individual B without providing any compensation to the victim. A variety of antipollution measures was proposed to deal with various forms of environmental abuse commonly encountered, each of which was designed to have the effect of making the would-be polluter bear the entire cost of whatever production or consumption activity he chose to engage in. Enactment and universal enforcement of a comprehensive set of such measures would make it unprofitable to commit any pollution trespass, and if any such act were committed by accident the injured party would have the right to full compensation. The effectiveness of none of these pollution control measures in any way depends on the population density of the region within which they are enforced. It is true that without pollution control, more population means more pollution. But a highway traveled by 1 million smog-free electric cars does not produce any more smog than a highway

25 September 27, 1970, Section E., p. 7.

traveled by one such car; the total amount of smog produced is zero in each case. If you want to control pollution, go at it directly, not via the back-door measure of population control.

Even if we were so clumsy as to try to control pollution by stopping population growth (remember burning down the barn to roast the pig?) we would fail in our objective. Conservationists who advocate this approach are guilty of one of the same fallacies as the chambers of commerce mentioned above, namely, that the economy will stop growing if population stops growing. In the opening paragraph of their book Rienow and Rienow write:

> Every 8 seconds a new American is born. He is a disarming little thing, but he begins to scream loudly in a voice that can be heard for seventy years. He is screaming for 56,000,000 gallons of water, 21,000 gallons of gasoline, 10,150 pounds of meat, 28,000 pounds of milk and cream, 9,000 pounds of wheat, and great storehouses of all other foods, drinks, and tobaccos. These are his lifetime demands on the economy.

Their implication is that if this child were not born, the 21,000 gallons of gasoline and other demands, plus all the concomitant refuse and pollution would never need to be produced. This is false, for the economy would keep right on growing without him. Most of the 21,000 gallons of gasoline would still be produced, but would not go to this child. Instead they would be split up in such a way as to increase the per capita gasoline consumption of the remaining population. As long as strong pollution control measures are not instituted to raise the ratio of Type I to Type ll GNP (see Chapter 1), our environment will just get dirtier and dirtier as time goes on, whether population growth stops or not.

This population-pollution fallacy is not the only conservationist argument for population control. A second is based on the phenomenon of pure crowding, external effects aside. Reducing this argument to its barest essentials, suppose two young married couples, the Campbells and the Schwartzes, are shipwrecked on a small, but quite habitable island in the middle of nowhere. Each couple looks forward with pleasure to the prospect of producing sons and daughters to perpetuate themselves, but in doing so, it is clear that a possible conflict between two factors exists. On the one hand, the total parental satisfaction of each couple would be greater, the greater the number of offspring in the family. On the other, their parental satisfaction per child, if you can conceive of measuring such a thing, will be less the less comfortable the conditions in which these children will have to live out their lives. Suppose the Campbells say to themselves, if the Schwartzes are going to have a large family the island will get pretty crowded, but if that's the way it's going to be, then we'd rather have four kids growing up on a crowded island than one or two kids growing up on a crowded island. If the Schwartzes reason the same way chances are the island will rapidly reach the level of overpopulation which we defined earlier as the "marginal subsistence solution".

Isn't this really foolish behavior for the islanders? Wouldn't they be better off getting together and making an agreement that each would have two children only, on the grounds that to have two children grow up to live a prosperous life is better than to have four grow up to live a life of strife and starvation? If such an agreement is beneficial for the islanders, doesn't the same reasoning apply to all the people of the United States? Wouldn't we all be better off sacrificing the small freedom of having a large family in return for the great benefit of having our small families grow up in an uncrowded environment?

It must be admitted that this line of reasoning does display a certain sophistication and theoretical elegance which surpasses anything we have encountered so far. In fact, it amounts to an entirely different approach to the question of the optimal population size. Instead of the absurdity of trying to find a single numerical value for population which would somehow be best for everyone, and which would then become the goal of government population policy, this line of reasoning attempts to justify collective action on behalf of population control by establishing that the invisible hand does not provide us with an efficient solution to the population size problem. And, as was demonstrated with the simplified example of the islanders, it is possible to imagine situations in which collectively agreeing upon some set of decisions concerning family size, other than those which would be made freely and independently, might be mutually beneficial to all members of the community.

The principal difficulty with this as a guide to practical population policy is that it is a sword which cuts both ways. Just put the Campbells and the Schwartzes on a very large island. Now the Campbells might reason as follows: "Each child which we raise will be an added expense for us, so we are reluctant to have more than a few. But we would like to see these children grow up in a community of sufficient size to provide a varied social life, the possibility for specialization in the division of labor, and the opportunity for cooperation in defense against jungle beasts. Therefore, let us propose an agreement with the Schwartzes that if they will have a few extra children to act as companions, mates, and helpers of ours, then we, in return, will bear the added expense of a few more children of our own." Returning from the island to the U.S., couldn't we find people saying, "Let us tax small families and subsidize large ones, each of us giving up the small amount of freedom implied in order that our children can grow up in a world where retail sales are stronger, and our country is a leading military power!"

If the free rider problem could be overcome, all the srnall-population advocates might conceivably agree mutually to restrict family size, and all the big-population advocates might agree mutually to expand family size. It is then rather difficult to see exactly what the outcome would be in a community where these two parties were anywhere near equal in numbers. Could an efficient, mutually beneficial arrangement be negotiated between the two groups? Perhaps members of each might band together and offer subsidies to members of the other to reverse their allegiance. This attempt would probably fail because some individuals would try to cheat, feigning the opposite of their true opinion in order to collect the subsidy from their fellows. It is difficult to believe that the hypothetically possible efficient move to a strictly voluntary collective population policy could ever be arranged in practice in a large community of widely divergent opinions.

We are left in a rather unsatisfactory position. We cannot hope to find a magic number optimal population target; yet we cannot rigorously establish that the population which results from free and individual decisions represents a state of efficiency, let alone of global optimality. It seems that we are left with the choice either of permitting one sub-group of the population to impose its favored population policy on the rest, against their will via the political process, or of pursuing a completely *laissez faire* population policy despite the theoretical difficulties which this will encounter. In practice, I favor the *laissez faire* approach, for two sound reasons. First, the *burden of proof* must always rest with the proponents of any positive action by the state which involves the restriction of the freedom of individuals, whether allegedly for their own good or not, and this burden of proof cannot now be met by the advocates either of population expansion or reduction. Second, it appears that if current demographic trends in the United States are left to work themselves out spontaneously, we will have a population with as reasonable characteristics of size and stability as any population target likely to be hammered out via the devious channels of demo-cratic choice and legislative compromise.

Commentary

What has changed

What happened to the population explosion that everyone was worried about in the 1970s? We can't really say that it didn't happen. The world's population did double between 1960 and 2000, the shortest doubling time in all of human history.

It would be more accurate to say that the population bomb did explode, but that we survived it. University of Michigan professor Donald Lam, in a presidential address to the Population Association of America, put it this way:

> The shift from large families making low investments in their children to small families making high investments in their children is a fundamental dimension of economic development during this period [1960-2010] . . . We put pressure on resources in ways we never had before. The challenges we face in future – while staggering – are nothing compared to what we've already gone through, and we have reasons to be optimistic about the future.[26]

Because of the trend toward smaller families noted by Lam, the world's population is unlikely ever to double again. The most probable scenario projected by the United Nations is for the world population to rise from its current level of around 7 billion today to around 10 billion by the end of the 21st century, and after that, to level off and gradually decline.

Ten billion is a lot of people. Some parts of the planet are already crowded, and will become more so. Even though endless doubling of the global population may not be in store, as some once feared, many observers still view any further population increase with dismay. To take a typical example, here is what John Bongaarts, a

---

[26] David Lam, preview of the PAA presidential address posted to the web site of the Population Studies Center of the University of Michigan. The posted document contains several interesting graphs that support the views expressed. See http://www.psc.isr.umich.edu/events/archive/2011/paa/david_lam.html .

demographer at the Population Council, had to say in response to the release of the most recent UN population projections: "Every billion more people makes life more difficult for everybody – it's as simple as that....[W]e obviously would be better off with a smaller population."[27]

Others challenge the view that a larger population necessarily makes everyone worse off. Probably the best-known exponent of the view that population growth is not all bad is Julian Simon, author of *The Ultimate Resource*.[28] Simon maintained that critics of population growth underestimate two important economic realities. One is the tendency of scarcity to lead to higher prices, which in turn lead to development of substitutes. The other is the importance of knowledge as a factor in economic development, so that more people mean more minds working to solve problems.

My own view is that the debate between population pessimists and Simonite optimists is beside the point. As the global population grows toward its eventual peak of 10 billion or so, we will undoubtedly see manifestations of both negative and positive externalities. The relative strengths of these tendencies are likely to vary widely from one region of the world to another, depending both on local variations in demographic trends and on the degree to which local policies support the kind of free-market environment that is needed to underpin the beneficial effects of population growth that Simon emphasized. Along the way, demographic changes will pose serious challenges for policy in the interrelated areas of environment, agriculture, and non-renewable resources. However things work out, among the existential risks that humanity faces, from war, to pestilence, to asteroid strikes, the risk of breeding ourselves to extinction seems to have receded.

Turning specifically to the U.S. demographic situation, the most recent doubling of the population took longer than the average for

---

27 Quoted in *The New York Times*, May 4, 2011. Justin Gillis and Cella W. Dugger, "U.N. Sees Rise For the World To 10.1 Billion," downloaded from http://www.nytimes.com/2011/05/04/world/04population.html?_r=1&scp=2&sq=gillis%20dugger%2010%20billion&st=cse

28 Princeton University Press, 1981.

the rest of the world – 60 years, from 1950 to 2010. There is still talk of a demographic crisis in the United States, but not one of exploding population. The original edition of this book cited predictions the U.S. net reproduction rate (NRR) would drop below the replacement level of 1.0 about 1975. In fact, it happened a little sooner. The NRR averaged just .96 for 1970-75 and dropped to an all-time low of .86 for the next ten years. By the turn of the century, it had risen back to almost exactly the replacement rate, where it is expected to stay. An NNR of 1.0 does not bring population growth to a halt immediately because of demographic momentum. It takes more than an entire human lifetime for the relative numbers of people of different ages in a population to reach an equilibrium. But even taking demographic momentum into account, the U.S.-born population is likely to stabilize by mid-century.

Rather than population growth, two other demographic issues are seen as greater policy headaches for the United States and most other industrialized countries in coming decades: the aging of the population and immigration.

A falling birthrate and longer life expectancies are bringing about a dramatic rise in the old-age dependency ratio. In 1970, there were 16 people aged 65 and older for each 100 people of working age. Today, the U.S. dependency ratio is 19, and by 2050 it will reach 35, based on current trends in mortality. In Europe, Japan, and China, the rise in old-age dependency ratios will be even faster. The rising dependency ratio will require major changes in budgetary policy. The twentieth-century U.S. fiscal model that permitted generous Medicare and social security benefits for all senior citizens, while federal taxes remained among the lowest in the developed world, will not survive the coming "grey tsunami". Either benefits will be cut, or taxes will rise, or the government will go broke. It is turning out to be difficult to decide which of these alternatives is the least unattractive.

Immigration is another thorny political issue. People in the rest of the world continue to see the United States, the European Union, and other wealthy countries as lands of opportunity. To some extent, immigration to these countries is a win-win situation. Immigration of young working-age people reduces a country's dependency ratio and can provide a bridge to a stable-population future. However, immigration policy is not just a matter of economics. There are limits to the rate at which societies can absorb immigrants without wrenching cultural disruptions.

However troublesome they may be, the policy issues raised by an aging population and immigration do not really fall within the scope of this book. They do not, *per se*, have major environmental implications. There is no particular reason to think, for a given total population, that one with a greater proportion of older people is worse for the environment than one with more younger people. Similarly, for a given total world population, there is no reason to think that a person has a bigger negative impact on the environment when he or she moves from a poor country to a rich one. True, the immigrant's income may increase after moving to the richer country, but that is offset, at least in part, by the fact that richer countries have better controls over pollution than poorer ones – a subject to which we will return in the next chapter.

What has not changed

What has not changed is that population growth, even if it is not as explosive as it was once feared to be, does pose real challenges for environmental policy. The more people, the more important it is to get things right in the relationship between people and the Spaceship Earth we live on. At least three issues require even closer attention as the population grows than they would with a constant population.

The first issue is pollution, both local (think of the smog in Beijing or Mexico City) and global (think climate change). If world population is going to increase another 50 percent before it reaches its eventual maximum, pollution per person will have to decrease by at least a third just to keep total pollution from getting worse. In the case of pollutants that are already above their sustainable level, the decrease per person will have to be even greater.

Achieving the needed decrease in pollution will be a challenge, but it need not be an insurmountable one. Consider CO_2 emissions, one of the most-watched types of pollution. For some time there has been a global downward trend of about 2 percent per year in CO_2 emissions per dollar of GDP. Three factors lie behind the trend. One is a shift to a service economy, for example, spending more on entertainment, less on clothing. Another is a shift to more energy-efficient technologies, for example, LED lighting and low-power computer chips. Still another is a shift to lower carbon energy sources, including fully renewable sources such as wind and solar and also bridge fuels such as natural gas and nuclear power. Despite these trends, achieving a decrease in total carbon output remains difficult, because GDP per capita and total population continue to increase.

As far as the United States goes, data for recent years suggest that the peak of carbon emissions per capita has passed, although it is not certain the trend will hold. There does not appear to be any technical reason why carbon emissions could not be reduced greatly, judging by the performance of other wealthy countries. Carbon emissions per capita in Japan and Norway are only half as high as in the United States, and they are only a third as high in France and New Zealand. What is needed is better policy, above all, policy that imposes the costs of pollution on the polluters themselves through higher prices. If all countries cut CO_2 output by the difference between the U.S. rate and the New Zealand rate, total world carbon emissions could fall by half even while world population grew to 10 billion people.

Non-renewable resources are a second problem that requires closer attention as population grows. We will return to resource depletion and its consequences in the next chapter, but a few comments are in order here. In the greater scheme of human development, we can look at the role of non-renewable resources as a bridge from a low-tech past, with short lifespans, high infant mortality, and a low standard of living, to a future with a higher quality of life based on sustainable technology. Since mineral deposits of any given quality are finite, more rapid population growth means that we must be that much more careful to make the best use of the resource bridge.

Doing so will require policies that encourage efficient use of non-renewable resources. Instead, resources are too often used wastefully. Wasteful use is especially likely when government policies encourage rapid development of non-renewable resources without placing the full costs of depletion, and of pollution associated with extraction, on the developers.

Development of offshore oil fields provides an example. The oil deposits are typically owned by governments and leased to private developers. Governments are often tempted to accelerate development in the name of ephemeral political goals, such as keeping fuel prices low before an upcoming election, if the country is democratic, or if it is not, grabbing a corrupt share of oil loot before some young colonel throws out the current aging despot and settles down for a little looting of his own. Sure signs of wasteful development of non-renewable resources include tax breaks for exploration and production, leases that do not reflect full depletion costs, and failure to impose the full costs of spills and pollution on producers.

The third problem that requires greater attention as population grows is management of local and global commons. The term *commons*, in this sense, refers to resources that are shared and to which everyone has unrestricted access. Local commons include things like public parks and local groundwater reservoirs. Global commons include, most importantly, the world's atmosphere and oceans.

More than 300 years ago, John Locke proposed that people living in a community have a right to take what they want from the commons only to the extent that in doing so, they leave as much and as good for others. That is a fine principle when the demand for use of the commons is low enough. There are still cases where that is true for local commons. You can still walk on the Oregon beaches (but not the Delaware beaches) and leave plenty of room for others, and you can still draw all the water you need for household use from wells in many (but not all) areas. However, as population density increases, there is necessarily a decrease in the prevalence of commons from which people can take what they need and still leave as much and as good for others.

When pressure on common resource reaches the point where whatever each person takes leaves less for others, unrestricted access becomes inconsistent with efficient use. Pastures are overgrazed, aquifers are pumped dry, fish stocks are depleted to the point of extinction. Then one of two solutions to the problem of overuse needs to come into play.

One is privatization. That solution has worked well for many once-common resources. The common pastures and woodlots that were open to European villagers in Locke's day were privatized through "enclosure" centuries ago. In U.S. history, Western grasslands that were once seen as a limitless commons for hunting and grazing were privatized through homesteading or other means. In many places, access rights to surface water and groundwater have also been privatized.

The alternative to privatization is common management for mutual benefit. Unfortunately, that mechanism has not always worked so well. Common management of forest land has often, in practice, been biased toward commercial uses such as logging at the expense of competing recreational and conservation interests. Attempts to manage ocean fisheries have often broken down either because governments give in to short-sighted political pressures for more fishing, or because fishing quotas are inadequately enforced. In some cases governments have achieved reasonable management of local and regional airsheds, but management of the global airshed against transnational pollutants has had few if any successes. A rare exception may be the Montreal Protocol for control of chloroflourocarbons that damage the earth's ozone layer.

Taking all of the above into account, we can summarize the relationship between population growth and the environment in these three propositions:

1. Without adequate controls over pollution, wise use of non-renewable resources, and rational management of local and global commons, the planet will face steady environmental degradation over the long term even without runaway population growth.
2. At the margin, population growth is not environmentally neutral; it increases the urgency of adopting sound environmental policies, including policies based on the principle that polluters and resource users pay in full for all environmental impacts.
3. There is a need to act but no need to panic. The world's human population is not, as once feared, on a track toward endless doublings. With sound policies in place, the world's expected peak population of 10 billion or so should be able to live together on our small planet in an environmentally sustainable manner.

Population pessimists often point out the physical impossibility of billions of Chinese and Indians ever enjoying today's American standard of living, by which they appear to mean driving the same number of miles per year in equally inefficient cars and eating the same annual quantity of cheeseburgers. People who think this way suffer from Imagination Deficit Disorder. Of course the future will not just be one of more people doing exactly what a few people are doing today. After all, today we do not, could not, and should not want to live as our ancestors did two centuries back, eating game killed in the local forests, using backyard outhouses for our sanitary needs, and burning whale oil in our lamps.

The future will be different from the present, and in most respects, it will be different in ways we cannot even imagine, just as has always been the case. Science fiction authors of the 19th century wrote about traveling to the moon in spacecraft made of brass and leather. Futurologists of the 1950s foresaw a world in which masses of people would commute to work in private helicopters, and computers would become an amazing 100 or 1,000 times more powerful, but would still fill gymnasium-sized buildings. (Even Heinlein's *Moon is a Harsh Mistress*, a visionary book in many respects, featured just such a computer.)

Despite the hazards of predicting the future, we can say with a fair degree of certainty that if markets are allowed to function, people in the future will use relatively less of things whose prices increase by more than the average. One thing that means is that as GDP grows, the long trend toward consumption of relatively more services and relatively fewer goods will continue. Another likely development is that if energy prices continue to rise, entrepreneurs will be encouraged to develop more energy-efficient lighting, transportation, and housing. In fact, some of that future technology is already available; its introduction is held back only by public policies that keep energy prices artificially low. As relative prices change, diets are likely to change, too. For example, barring unforeseen changes in farm technology, it is likely that rising global incomes will cause an increase in the price of meat relative to the price of plant-based foods. If so, people in the future will probably eat less meat than people in rich countries do today, and will very likely live healthier lives as a result.

In closing, let me say that I realize some readers will find my comments here excessively optimistic, just as I find my own comments of 40 years ago excessively pessimistic. I know there are people who continue to think that a "population bomb" poses a threat to humankind. I know, too, that there are "deep ecologists" who think that people themselves are a form of pollution, and who would like to see a human population no larger than could live as hunter-gatherers, with no agriculture, mining, or industry whatsoever. [29]

I also encounter people who support proactive government policies to reduce birthrates. Some people still favor something like the Chinese one-child policy, despite all its unintended consequences, from forced abortion to female infanticide, and despite

---

[29] See, for example, the article on deep ecology in the *Encyclopedia of Earth*, an on-line, peer-reviewed publication, http://www.eoearth.org/article/Deep_ecology.

the fact that the Chinese themselves seem to be quietly backing away from it as unworkable and unneeded. If the only alternatives facing the human race were a one-child policy or endless population doublings, I could understand why someone might choose the former. However, if what we are really facing is one final 50 percent increase before global peak population is reached, I prefer policies that reduce units of pollution per person rather than those that aim to reduce persons per unit of pollution.

Finally, let me say that in continuing to favor a *laissez faire* population policy, I fully endorse continued vigorous efforts to ensure that reproductive choices are made by people who are free and informed. We are not yet at that point. Many children are born to women who are coerced by men, who have restricted access to resources for family planning, or who are too poorly educated to make informed choices. The experience of many nations shows that when barriers to free and informed reproductive choices are lifted, fertility rates fall. All indications are that prosperous, free, and informed parents do not, on average, have more children than are consistent with an indefinitely sustainable human population. By all means, we should do everything we can to make sure those conditions become universal.

Chapter 6

ENVIRONMENTAL PROBLEMS AND ECONOMIC DEVELOPMENT

Even the idea of attempting to discuss the subject of economic development in one small chapter must seem ludicrous to any reader who has seen the long shelves of books on the topic housed in the average university library stacks. Anyone familiar with the content and not just the number of such books will doubtless be more skeptical still, for the notorious tendency of economists to be unable to agree on a single matter of theory or policy is even more pronounced among development specialists than in the rest of the profession. Nonetheless the attempt must be made, for those long, subtle chains of cause and effect upon which the science of ecological economics focuses its attention have a disturbing way of sneaking across national frontiers and across the boundaries that separate the "developed" from the "underdeveloped" world.

In order to keep from drifting too far away from our main topic this chapter will be limited to a consideration of the ways in which specifically environmental aspects of the development problem relate to the conduct of American policy toward developing countries. Within these self-imposed limits, the two most important problem areas concern world trade in natural resources and the population explosion in the underdeveloped world.

Are We Exploiting the Third World?

One of the statistical tidbits frequently encountered in the numerous popular books available on the environmental crisis is that the United States, with some 6 percent of the world's population, consumes a vastly greater percentage than this of the world's raw materials. Figures for individual products can be calculated with a fair degree of accuracy, for example, a fourth of all the world's potash (and beer), a third of all tin, half of all newsprint. Aggregate statistics are a good deal less reliable, but range from 30 to 50 percent of *all* the world's non-renewable natural resources of *all* kinds. A great and increasing fraction of this total is imported from developing countries. The U.S. imports virtually all of its chrome, cobalt, manganese, nickel, and tin; about half of its lead, tungsten, and zinc; and increasingly large quantities of products of which it has long been considered a leading producer, such as oil, iron ore, and copper.

Could it be that we are taking more than our fair share of these things? Do the statistics on the flow of natural resources from the underdeveloped to the developed world imply an exploitation of the former by the latter? What do we mean by "exploitation" anyway? Are we appropriating resources without giving just compensation? Does our resource consumption pattern hinder the development of third world trading partners?

Before leaping to any conclusions in answer to these questions the reader would be well-advised to pause and apply his now extensive knowledge of economic theory to the matter of trade between nations. He will discover that the simple fact of our large primary product imports does not, standing by itself, indicate that anyone is being exploited. At first glance the exact opposite might more likely be indicated.

What we call trade is nothing more than the common organizational means used to extract the potential for mutual benefit from a situation of economic inefficiency. It would be inefficient for the butcher to have all those hundreds of pounds of meat and for me to have none, so we trade, and both profit thereby. If either he or I were to propose an exchange on the basis of terms of trade which were not mutually beneficial, I would choose to become a vegetarian or he would choose to retain excess inventories rather than engage in a transaction that left either of us less well off than before. Juxtaposition of the terms "exploitation" and "free trade" represents self-contradiction.

Mutual gains are as much a natural result of trade between the United States and the developing world as between the butcher and me. The gains to the U.S. are obvious. Our huge industrial machine and astronomical (by world historical measures) standard of living gobble up huge doses of materials which we either cannot produce, or cannot produce cheaply, at home. Without them, our output and consumption could not be maintained at the present levels with current technology.

The advantage gained from trade by the developing country is usually thought of in terms of an opportunity for accelerated economic growth rather than simply for increased current consumption (although the latter would also be possible). Let us consider a country rich in oil. Even without world trade a country with good oil resources would have a distinct advantage in development, being able to use the product in many ways as a lubricant, a fuel, and the source of a huge variety of synthetic materials, even synthetic food. At first the amount of oil used would be small, for the equipment to extract it, refine it, transport it, and be lubricated and fueled by it would have to be painstakingly accumulated step by step on the basis of the primitive industrial establishment and limited investment potential of the home country. Trade offers an obvious shortcut to development. An oil-hungry developed nation, already having depleted its own supplies, might be willing to trade sophisticated industrial plant and equipment for the oil which the underdeveloped country could not use in any event until the distant future.

The oil producing country is faced with a clear choice: It can leave future generations struggling to pull themselves up by their own bootstraps atop a sea of petroleum reserves, or it can present these same future citizens with a modernized, prosperous economy, running low on oil but equipped with the technological and industrial flexibility to diversify its energy base to suit these conditions. If the latter path is chosen, members of those future generations will thank today's decision makers for permitting the greedy trading partner to swallow up far more than its share of the world oil reserves, for look what they got in return!

Despite the logical appeal of this line of argument, and despite the existence of many instances in which things have worked out more-or-less along these lines, we cannot leave the matter here. For although it may be true that developing nations can potentially benefit from the export of their natural resources to industrialized regions, for a variety of reasons they do not always succeed in realizing their end of the potential mutual gains from trade. Let us see why this is so.

First, it happens that export of raw materials is a shortcut to development only under the condition that export earnings are wisely and productively invested in development activities. But if underdeveloped countries were equipped with efficient governments, thrifty propertied classes, and armies of dynamic indigenous entrepreneurs, they would not still be underdeveloped today! The literature on development economics is jam packed with horror stories of lavish presidential palaces, rows of diplomats' Mercedes, fat numbered Swiss bank accounts, jet planes and submarines bought as playthings to payoff soldier-politicians – all purchased out of earnings from the export of the nation's irreplaceable patrimony of natural resources. Small wonder the term "kleptocracy" has been coined to describe the political system of these unfortunate lands where the government gets gaudier and gaudier as the nation gets poorer and poorer. More sobering still is the fact that even honest and prudent governments, in the countries lucky enough to have them, are not always able to avoid errors, misconceptions, and blind alleys in development planning which also waste many hard-earned resources.

If the people of the developing nations are being exploited by their own domestic regimes, it might be maintained that the alleged imperialist powers which trade with them are not at fault and that the victims have only themselves to blame if they do not throw the rascals out. This might be a telling argument, were it not for the realities of cold war politics. All too often honest and capable leaders are left to languish while Moscow and Washington lavish diplomatic, military, and economic support on their corrupt client dictatorships and plot to oust one another's kleptocratic puppets. The third world might well be hindered in its development by this kind of "trade."

Second, the doctrine that world commerce in primary products is beneficial to both the developed and developing partners is robbed of much of its force unless that trade is genuinely free trade. Unfortunately, free trade is a principle all too often honored in the breach. The very fact that trade so frequently takes the form of sales and negotiations between governments, rather than directly between individual citizens of different countries, is a clear indication of this fact. Even trade among governments is not free, but encumbered by an incredible network of tariffs, quotas, split exchange rates, tie-in sales, taxes, subsidies, restrictions, and regulations. It is often charged, and not easy to disprove, that the domination of the world trade and monetary systems by a handful of industrial powers is used to keep raw material prices low and sources of supply open.

We have not yet mentioned the grossest violation of free trade – the immigration restrictions (and in certain well-known cases, emigration restrictions as well) enforced by virtually every state on the surface of the globe. How can the governments of rich countries claim to have the interests of the poor of the underdeveloped world at heart if they insist on preventing their own employers from offering work to the unemployed of other nations? I think any American who speaks altruistically of stepping up our foreign aid, and at the same time grows rich behind our severe immigration barriers, deserves a nomination for hypocrite of the month.

Finally, an element of truth may be discovered in the arguments of those who charge neocolonial exploitation, if we stop to consider the "advantages of coming second" in comparison to "the advantages of coming first." Second-comers, we are often told, have the tremendous developmental advantage of being able to borrow from the technology of those who came first. (Just think what a great advantage it would have been for the U.S., Britain, or Germany if a little green man in a flying saucer touched down in the year 1790 or so, and had patiently explained the Bessemer process for making steel!) Yet the advantages of developing in a world full of advanced technology could be offset for latecomers by a matching disadvantage – that of growing up in a world where all those export earnings and all that wizard technology had to be harnessed to synthesizing once-abundant natural products and to processing abysmally low-grade ores at astronomical expense.

Imagine that the munificent beneficence of international capitalism has provided the oil-exporting nation of our previous example with a huge, modern refinery, all paid for out of royalties and export earnings. When the last oil has been pumped up from beneath the sands will a "fourth world" suddenly appear from which this country can import its raw materials? Or will the refinery be left as a huge rusting white elephant in the desert, while its highly trained but narrowly specialized labor force goes back to herding camels?

Ultimately, a study of the dismal science of ecological economics leads one to the conclusion that the second-comers had best begin thinking of some alternative future for themselves other than economic "development" as defined by the example of the first-comers. Development in the past has simply meant growth of Type II GNP, but the prospects for bringing the entire world up to the present American level of industrialization on the basis of a throughput technology are virtually nil. There just are not enough sources and sinks in the world to do it. Sooner or later both developed and underdeveloped countries will be forced to make the transition to an ecologically viable economy.[30] There can be no doubt that learning to live within the limits of one's environment will be a harder task for the poor than for the rich to face.

To summarize, although the simple belief that a nation is being exploited unless it is allowed to keep all of its manganese ore for domestic consumption appears to be a serious oversimplification, it must be admitted that the policies, and sometimes simply the existence, of industrialized countries often make life more difficult than it need be for the second-comers. Whether the label of "imperialist exploitation" is or is not applied to what has gone on in the past is relatively unimportant. The important task for development economics now is to begin thinking about the future and how the third world can learn to cope with problems of population, resources, and environment from which we Americans miraculously escaped in the course of our own growth from poverty to prosperity.

---

30 Chapter 8 of this book contains a discussion of what such an economy might look like.

Population, Loaves, and Fishes

In the last chapter we came to the guardedly optimistic conclusion that the population of the United States may be expected in time to level off at a figure which would permit a standard of living well above the subsistence level.[31]

The question now is whether a similar optimism is justified with respect to the demographic situation in developing countries. The answer is *no*. The crucial difference lies in a relationship between population growth and the level of development called the *demographic transition*.

The phenomenon of the demographic transition can be easily understood by looking at Figure 6.1. Section A shows how birth and death rates respond to the process of economic development. At a very low level of development both birth and death rates are high. As the process of development begins, increasing prosperity makes better nutrition and medical care available. This brings about a drop in the death rate. Economic development also affects the birth rate, but not in such a simple and rapid fashion. It takes considerable time for the complex effects of cultural change, the spread of literacy and education, increasing urbanization, and other factors to have any impact on the birth rate. Eventually, as the transition to a modern industrialized, urbanized society is completed, the birth rate falls, narrowing the gap between births and deaths once again.

Part of the figure shows what happens to the rate of population growth during the process of demographic transition. Since, as will be recalled, the rate of population growth at a given moment is calculated as the difference between the Crude Birth Rate and Crude Death Rate, population growth is low both at very low and

---

[31] Certain assumptions were necessary to support this, and violation of any one of them might upset the conclusion. It was necessary to assume that current trends in reproductive behavior would not sharply reverse themselves; that the government would have the wisdom to abstain from active promotion of population growth; and that the programs for pollution abatement, wilderness preservation, and so on set forth in other sections of this book would be implemented; since without these it is difficult for our environment to contain even our present population comfortably.

very high levels of development. During the transitional phase, when "death control" has taken effect and birth control has not, population grows explosively. As a result the curve relating population growth to economic development has a distinct hump in the middle.

Figure 6.1 The demographic transition

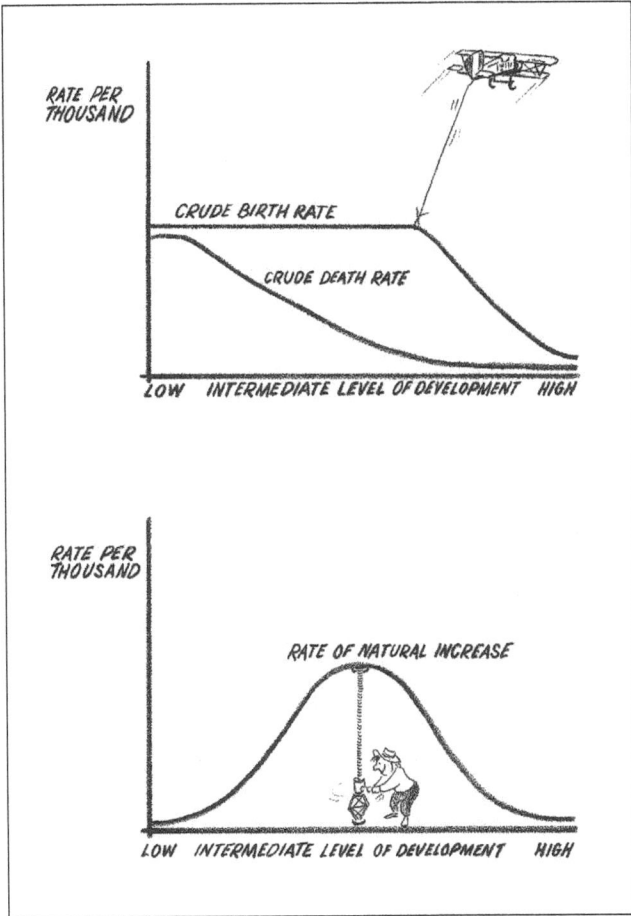

It is this hump which is the primary cause of pessimism concerning the population problem in developing countries. It would be nice if we could be sure that in time the natural course of events would carry these nations through, as happened in the past to all of today's already developed nations. Unfortunately, getting over the hump may be more difficult in the future than it was in the past.

For one thing the hump is higher than it used to be. America and Western Europe underwent the demographic transition in the last century in a period when medical technology was in a very primitive state as compared to today. Thus the death rate curve fell neither so soon, so sharply, nor so far as in the 20th century when Western medicine has been imported wholesale into the third world, sometimes cutting the death rate by more than half in a single decade.

Today's higher hump raises the ominous possibility that countries caught to the left of it may get stuck in a "population trap" and never make it over at all. This could happen because rising population growth lowers the rate of growth of per capita income, even while the growth rate of GNP in absolute terms continues at a constant rate. If population growth catches up to the rate of growth of GNP, "development" in any meaningful sense ceases and poverty is simply reproduced on a larger and larger scale each year.

In addition to the danger of the population trap, developing countries today face the prospect that time is simply running out for them. The developed nations could afford a hundred years or more to work their way at a leisurely pace through the demographic transition. In those days a new continent was being opened, and a seemingly limitless abundance of sources and sinks permitted "quick and dirty" throughput methods of industrialization. Neither time, space, nor resources will permit a repetition of this process on a world-wide scale now.

Given this difficult situation, what policy alternatives are available to us and to the leaders of the developing nations themselves? The available alternatives were succinctly expressed more than a century ago by John Stuart Mill:

Society can feed the necessitous if it takes their multiplication under control, or (if destitute of all moral feeling for the wretched offspring) it can leave the last to their discretion, abandoning the first to their own care. But it cannot with impunity take the feeding upon itself, and leave the multiplying free.[32]

Many observers of world population and development today seem to be suffering from a sort of "omnipotence complex" which prevents them from making a reasoned choice among Mill's three alternatives. Just as many Pentagon strategists suffer from the delusion that there is no limit to what American military power can accomplish by way of influencing the course of world politics, these people think that there is no limit to the ability of American industry, agriculture, and technology to shape the course of world economic development. Observing the tendency of world population to grow at geometric rates, they leap to the conclusion that we "must" somehow feed all those additional people who are on their way into the world; and from there, they leap to the still more fantastic conclusion that we not only "must" but *can* do this.

In effect, these people are proposing that we plunge ahead into the third alternative, hoping for some sort of miracle of loaves and fishes to save us from the consequences. As Mill clearly foresaw, in warning against this policy, the only effect of pursuing it would be to activate the "utterly dismal theorem," and to insure that world population would in the end reach the absolute subsistence, rather than the marginal subsistence, level with everyone reduced to a common denominator of misery.

Many other would-be policy advisers, seeing the folly of pursuing this third alternative, opt for the first instead. They advocate undertaking the task of feeding those who cannot feed themselves, but, recognizing that loaves and fishes are available only in finite quantities, advocate taking "multiplication" under control

---

32 J. S. Mill, *Principles of Political Economy* (New York: Appleton, Century, Crofts, 1881), p. 447. Cited in John M. Culbertson, *Economic Development, An Ecological Approach* (New York: Alfred A. Knopf, 1971), Chapter 4.

at the same time. With this approach they hope to avoid both the marginal and absolute subsistence equilibria, hastening the world to the prosperous zone of population stability lying to the right of the population hump.

Examination of current and past programs undertaken to curb population growth in developing countries leads one to conclude that these people too must be suffering from an omnipotence complex. The idea that an army of American peace corpsmen, armed with shiploads of IUDs and contraceptive pills, can change the reproductive habits of two-thirds of the world's population overnight is about as realistic as it was to think that 100,000 U.S. Marines would be able to win a quick and decisive military victory in Vietnam. I do not want to belittle totally the importance of such efforts at birth control as have been undertaken, but merely to emphasize that their actual impact has been very small so far in comparison to the magnitude of the global problem, and that at best their effects on population growth are felt only over a long period.

To predict that we will be unable to accomplish miracles does not preclude a discussion of how the limited amount of aid which will presumably be forthcoming from developed countries might best be put to use. It is an important principle of economics that the less of something there is, the more care must be taken in allocating it. In this connection one of the most sensible suggestions which I have run across is that made by William and Paul Paddock, who advocate using the principle of "triage" to allocate future aid to developing nations.[33] Battlefield doctors, following the triage principle, refuse to treat either those who are in pain but will survive without treatment, or those who will die no matter what treatment they receive. Instead, they concentrate their limited facilities exclusively on those who would respond to care but would die without. By analogy, the Paddocks recommend concentrating all aid on those marginal countries which might just be able to make it over the hump, but only with outside help. They reason that it is wasteful to devote any aid to those who are already on the downhill run, even though they will suffer certain hardships before completing

[33] See *Famine 19751* (Boston: Little, Brown & Company, 1967).

their development. It is equally wasteful to help those who would not be able to escape the population trap despite our maximum efforts. By helping only the middle group, at least we can hope that our attempts to do good will actually do at least some good.

Yet what will become of those nations written off as hopeless? I suppose that there is some possibility of undue pessimism, and that the "green revolution" will succeed in carrying even these nations through the demographic transition without excessive difficulties. (Still, I cannot see that any harm will be done by preparing for the worst now.)

More likely, the latter part of this century will witness some instances of the massive riots, plagues, and famines foreseen by the prophets of doom. If such events do come to pass, it is at least possible that they will cure, by a sort of cruel shock treatment, the problems which the cold war competition in foreign aid cannot hope to resolve. In the end the abrupt rise in death rates and disorder predicted by the pessimists may ironically turn out to be the instrument for achieving the hope of the optimists, namely, an acceleration of social and cultural change resulting in a declining birth rate and a rude completion of the demographic transition.

Perhaps the reader will be disappointed by my suggestion that there is little or nothing we can do about the population explosion in underdeveloped countries. The sad fact is that we live in a world in which some problems exist which simply do not have tidy solutions waiting to be discovered by the inquiring mind of man. Given the realities of the situation, I think that the best we can do is to avoid being misguided by false hopes into undertaking policies which will do more harm than good.

True, widely held precepts of morality demand that we heal the sick and feed the hungry, but can we do this if the only result will be to increase the number of sick and hungry to be cared for in the next round? As one writer put it, "If ethical principles deny our right to do evil in order that good may come, are we justified in doing good when the forseeable consequence is evil?"[34]

---

34 A. V. Hill, in Hardin, *op. cit.*, p. 78.

Commentary

What has changed

This chapter, as written in 1971, was deeply pessimistic about prospects for economic development. Development remains a difficult and uncertain process and in some countries, it is not happening at all. Still, in at least some respects, the outlook is more hopeful than it was 40 years ago.

As discussed in the preceding chapter, the demographic situation is one thing that looks a little better, both for the world as a whole and for most countries taken individually. In 1970, China's population was doubling every 25 years and India's every 30 years. Today both countries are in the last stages of their demographic transitions. China's absolute population is expected to peak within 20 years, and India's net reproduction rate will have fallen below the replacement level by that time. In coming decades, it is likely that the rising old-age dependency ratios that come with rapidly slowing population growth will be a problem for more developing countries. At the same time, countries such as Yemen and Ethiopia, where fertility rates have not declined and population growth remains rapid, will increasingly be the exceptions.

As many formerly poor countries in Asia have moved into middle- and upper-income status, concerns about global poverty focus on a "bottom billion" who have been left behind. As Paul Collier points out in his book by that title, the poorest billion people in the world are concentrated in a group of countries, more of them in Africa than anywhere else, that face one or more of four great handicaps: war, bad government, landlocked geography, and problems stemming from natural resources.[35] Because those countries have been left behind as others have developed, income inequality among nations has increased over the past forty years, even while income inequality for the world population as a whole has

---

[35] Paul Collier, *The Bottom Billion*, Oxford University Press, 2007.

decreased.[36] That result has disappointed many economists who expected poorer countries to catch up with rich ones by borrowing capital and technology.

On the other hand, not all the news is bad, even for the bottom billion. As Charles Kenny explains in his book, *Getting Better*, non-income measures of the quality of life have been improving even in countries where per capita GDP has stagnated.[37] For example, in 1950, life expectancy in the poorest 20 percent of countries was only about half that in the richest 20 percent. Today, people in the poorest countries live two-thirds as long as those in the richest countries. Similar trends have taken place in infant mortality. Even the AIDS epidemic has not prevented the gradual convergence of longevity and infant mortality between rich and poor countries.

Kenny notes similar progress in education. From 1950 to 2000, the share of the world's population who could read and write increased from about half to four-fifths. Over the same period, the literacy rate in the poorest 20 percent of countries rose from one-eighth of the rate in the richest 20 percent to half the rate of the richest. Women's literacy rates increased even faster over the period, rising from a global average of less than two-thirds that of men to around four-fifths that of men by the end of the twentieth century.

Why has life become less miserable for even the world's poorest populations? It may not be literally true that the best things in life are free, but it does appear that some of the good things in life have gotten cheaper. That is especially true for some the most basic inputs to good health, including clean water, sanitation, vaccines, and antibiotics.

---

36 Xavier Sala-i-Martin, "The Disturbing 'Rise' in Global Income Inequality," NBER Working Paper No. 8904, April 2002. The decrease in across-country inequality of the global population is largely due to the rapid growth of per capita income in China, a result that is somewhat paradoxical in view of the fact that income inequality within China has increased with growth. The author notes that if per capita income in Africa continues to grow as slowly as it has in the recent past, global across-country inequality will begin to rise again in coming decades.

37 Charles Kenny, *Getting Better*, Basic Books, 2011.

The upturn in health and education indicators does not mean that the job of development is finished. Kenny is very careful to emphasize that we must work even harder to improve things much more. However, the gains in infant mortality and education are important, especially for demographic reasons. A higher expectation that children will survive into adulthood removes an important economic incentive for large families in societies where parents must depend on their children for support in old age. Also, against cultural backgrounds of every kind, women who are more educated tend to have fewer children. Almost everywhere in the world, there is a clear connection between better health and education for the very poor and decreases in fertility rates.

One final ground for at least guarded optimism comes from research into the relationship between economic growth and environmental degradation. Since the early 1990s, researchers have repeatedly documented a tendency for pollution first to increase and then to decrease again as GDP per capita increases. This inverted-U pattern of increasing, then decreasing pollution is called the *environmental Kuznets curve* because of its resemblance to a similar relationship between income and inequality that was earlier discussed by Simon Kuznets.[38]

Evidence for the environmental Kuznets curve appears to be strongest for local air and water pollution. Examples of the Kuznets curve in action for the United States include the abatement of the once-notorious Los Angeles smog, and the restoration of Lake Erie, not yet pristine but much healthier than in the past. It also appears to hold strongly for deforestation.

For other pollutants, for loss of species, and for some other forms of environmental harms the environmental Kuznets curve is more controversial. Greenhouse gas (GHG) emissions are a case in point. Although GHG per unit of GDP does tend to decrease as income increases, it has not yet decreased rapidly enough to reduce

---

[38] For a brief review of the literature, see Arik Levinson, "Environmental Kuznets Curve," *New Palgrave Dictionary of Economics*, 2nd ed, 2008. The entry can be found on line at http://www9.georgetown.edu/faculty/aml6/pdfs&zips/PalgraveEKC.pdf

total emissions. That could mean that there is no inverted-U curve for GHG, or it could also mean that there is such a curve, but even wealthy countries have not yet reached the peak. Also, there may be a lag between the time rising income creates a demand for reductions in carbon emissions, and the time when research and development delivers the technologies needed to satisfy the demand. Even more importantly, it is to be hoped that over time rising income will lead to a demand for effective policies to control pollution of all kinds – policies that adhere to the TANSTAAFL principle.

What has not changed

One thing that has not changed is that for many countries, natural resource riches remain a barrier, rather than a path, to development. That fact, popularly known as "the curse of riches", was brought to wide attention in a 1995 paper by Jeffrey Sachs and Andrew Warner.[39] Sachs and Warner showed that over the period from 1960 to 1995, there was a systematic tendency for countries with abundant natural resources (measured by the share of natural resource export in total exports) to grow more slowly than those with fewer natural resources. The fastest growing countries in that period were resource-poor "Asian tigers" such as Taiwan and Singapore. Many of the countries with the greatest natural resource exports, such as Zaire (as the Democratic Republic of Congo was then known) and Ivory Coast actually experienced negative growth rates.

That is not how things should be. Natural resources should be a blessing that facilitates growth, not a curse that undermines it. Faster growth, in turn, should be good for the environment. Faster economic growth should accelerate the improvements in health and education that allow countries to move through the demographic transition to a new equilibrium with low birthrates, low death rates, and fertility rates no higher than the replacement level. Faster economic growth should also provide the capital needed for improved sanitation, more widespread recycling, greater energy

---

39   Jeffrey D. Sachs and Andrew M. Warner, "Natural Resource Abundance and Economic Growth," NBER Working Paper 5398, 1995

efficiency, and a transition to renewable energy sources. Those, in turn, are the changes needed to move a country past the peak of the environmental Kuznets curve and down the other side to full sustainability.

As discussed in earlier chapters, those processes do not always work as smoothly as they should, even in developed economies. A major reason they do not is the widespread failure of policies to adhere to the TANSTAAFL principle. Government policies of the "Drill Baby, Drill" variety encourage overly rapid extraction of non-renewable resources by failing to impose depletion costs on producers and consumers. Legal systems and regulations fail to protect property rights or force polluters to pay for the damage they do. No workable mechanisms are put in place to control exploitation of shared resources such as oceans and the global airshed. Much more can and should be done to improve environmental quality even in those countries that have escaped the curse of riches – countries like the United States, Canada, and Australia where natural resource wealth and economic growth have gone hand in hand.

In many poor countries, however, things have gone wrong in a much more fundamental way. Resources have been plundered without any resulting development. High infant mortality and lack of education have meant continued high fertility and rapid population growth. The kinds of environmental damage associated with poverty and economic stagnation have gone unchecked: deforestation, overhunting of endangered wildlife, habitat destruction, water pollution, unsanitary waste disposal, heavy air pollution from inefficient cooking fires, and more.

Consider the case of Equatorial Guinea. That tiny African country has a population of only 540,000, but oil production of 240,000 barrels a day, giving it a per capita GDP of more than $50,000 – the third highest in the world, adjusted for differences in cost of living. But Equatorial Guinea ranks 116th out of 175 countries on the U.N.'s Human Development Index, a measure that emphasizes health, education, and income per capita. Life expectancy is under

50 years. The unemployment rate is 30 percent. In short, the country is a poster child for the curse of riches.

More than anything, Equatorial Guinea suffers from bad governance. Its president, Obiang Nguema, seized power in a coup in 1979. He has diverted a substantial part of the country's oil wealth to his own personal use, and much of the rest of it to corrupt cronies who help him maintain his position. Not surprisingly, the country ranks very low on international measures of quality of governance. Freedom House gives it a rating of 7, the worst possible, on both human rights and political rights. Transparency International ranks it the 168th most corrupt country out of 178 surveyed. As a place to start a business, the World Bank ranks it the 179th worst country out of 183 surveyed.

Equatorial Guinea is not unique in suffering the combination of resource riches, bad governance, and lack of development. The problem seems to be worst in countries that have "point source" resource wealth, that is, concentrated natural resources such as oil or diamonds that can be easily monopolized. (Wealth from more widely dispersed natural resources such as land good for growing corn or coffee is harder to capture.) Point-source resource wealth, in turn, enables a political model based on patronage politics.[40] In such a system, the ruler's objective is, first, to stay in power, and second, to get rich. In order to do so, the country's resource wealth is used to finance a security apparatus that keeps rivals at bay, and at the same time, to buy off powerful regional, ethnic, religious, or business leaders. To keep the model going, institutions of political accountability, like independent courts, legislatures, a free press, and non-governmental organizations need to be kept weak.

A simpler name for the patronage politics model based on natural resource wealth is *kleptocracy* – literally, rule by thieves. Kleptocracy takes on its most spectacular forms in countries like Equatorial Guinea or Mobutu's Zaire, where the economy, outside

---

[40] For a discussion of the patronage politics model, see Paul Collier and Anke Hoeffler, "Resource Rents, Governance, and Conflicts," *Journal of Conflict Resolution*, Aug. 2005.

the resource sector, remains completely undeveloped. However, some features of the model can be found in more industrial countries that have vast resource wealth, for example, in Vladimir Putin's Russia or Nursultan Nazerbaev's Kazakhstan. Countries like Norway, which has managed to combine natural resource wealth with balanced economic development, democracy, rule of law, and respect for the environment, are the exceptions.

Can anything be done to break the grip of the curse of riches in the developing world? Perhaps. One approach, favored by international bodies such as the U.N. and the World Bank, has been to make development aid contingent on improvements in governance. Backers of this approach claim it sometimes works. Ghana will be a case to watch. Aid agencies cite it as an example of a country where economic development has been accompanied by an improvement in institutions of government. A test lies ahead, however. Large oil reserves have recently been discovered off Ghana's coast. Will its political institutions be strong enough to manage the oil wealth, or will the country slip backwards toward kleptocracy?

There is another policy change that wealthy countries, especially the United States, could use to break the curse of riches in the developing world. That would be to make sure that their own consumers of natural resources bear the full opportunity cost of their production and use. In the United States, prices of gasoline at the pump are nowhere near high enough to cover the environmental costs either of extracting or burning the fuel. Think of devastating oil spills in Nigeria's delta region. Think of the constantly rising CO_2 content of the atmosphere. A carbon tax, a cap-and-trade regime, an effective system of tort law that would allow victims of pollution to get redress in US courts would make a big difference. The price at the pump would go up, discouraging demand. Falling demand would push down the world market price for oil at the same time the price to consumers rose. A lower world oil price would undermine the revenue streams that kleptocratic third-world rulers use to maintain their systems of patronage politics.

Would such a policy solve all the problems of developing nations? Far from it. Many, if not most of their problems will require major reforms at home. But economically rational and environmentally sustainable policies by resource users would at least be a step in the right direction.

Chapter 7
PRESERVING THE WILDERNESS – PUBLIC INTEREST OR SPECIAL INTEREST?

Searching finance

On Good Economics and Good Government

In Chapter 4 it was argued that the use of general tax revenue to finance projects offering special benefits to a fraction of the population is both bad economics and bad government. It is bad economics since, except in the limiting case where all political decisions are made under the rule of unanimity, each such project will generally be funded beyond the point where the marginal cost of the project equals its marginal benefit. The necessary conditions for efficiency are violated and misallocation of resources results. The use of public funds for such projects is also bad government, because the non-beneficiary taxpayers are forced to invest a part of their earnings in a way which at best yields them no returns and, more often, causes them positive harm.

Get any good conservationist into a discussion on the subject of the Army Corps of Engineers or the Department of Highways and you will find an ardent supporter of this idea. He will curse the incredible waste and corruption involved in the history of massive federal giveaways to lumbering, mining, grazing, hydroelectric, and construction interests, and then curse them again because he as a taxpayer has been forced not only to suffer from the results of these criminal actions but actually to finance his own suffering!

If you really want to see some fireworks, ask this same conservationist if these same principles of government apply to such projects as national parks and wilderness preservation programs. Ask him why it is that if justice requires motorists to pay for their own roads, hydroelectric firms to pay for their own dams, golfers to pay for their own golf courses, and gourmets to pay for their own escargots, lovers of the wilderness should not pay for their own wilderness and campers for their own campsites? Why should the special interests of conservationists be subsidized by the taxes of non-conservationists?

You would be well advised to wear a verbal flak vest while asking this question, because your conservationist interlocutor is armed with quite an arsenal of replies. Let's devote a few pages to an examination of these replies.

I, too, am a wilderness lover, a member of the beneficiary group of conservation legislation, and you may be sure that I have asked these hard questions of myself a good many times and that I am really going to make sure that we sift these replies for any possible shred of a valid argument. I will also suggest some guidelines for a much more effective wilderness preservation program than the National Park system, one which is within the bounds of both good economics and good government.

Conservation and the Public Interest

The first gambit of the conservationist in defending public financing of his favorite projects is to argue that conservation and wilderness preservation is not a special interest at all, but, instead, the common interest of the whole population. This contention is without basis in fact. In the absence of strong evidence to the contrary, it seems safe to assume that the distribution of the populace with respect to their degree of interest in wilderness preservation looks something like the curve shown in Figure 7.1. The horizontal scale represents the degree of an individual's interest in wilderness preservation. Toward the right are located the real hard core enthusiasts. These include the 12,000 rugged devotees who visited Rainbow Bridge in the first fifty years after its discovery, making the difficult trip up or down river or twenty-eight miles overland by horseback. Somewhat to the left of them come the average backpacker whom one meets along sections of trail more, let us say, than five miles from the nearest road. Further toward the middle are the hundreds of thousands who make a visit to some of our more developed and accessible parks for a weekend or two out of the year, those who appreciate the wilderness through the window of a car, or who are content to patronize a modest state park near their home. At the extreme left of the scale are those who not only get no benefit from the wilderness but view it with positive displeasure, those who look at a tree and think what a waste that it has not yet been turned into a lovely residence or a page of their favorite magazine.

Figure 7.1 Hypothetical distribution of the population with respect to their interest in wilderness preservation

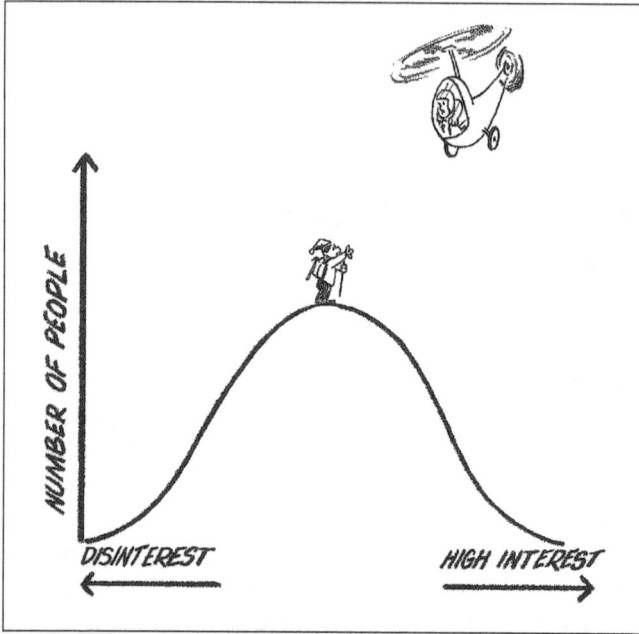

I will make no pretense at putting numbers on the vertical scale or dollar values along the horizontal, but we may be certain that this is a reality: a few people who benefit enormously from our national parks, a great many who derive a moderate benefit, and a few who are positively upset at the thought of a tree looking at a tree.

If the tax burden is assumed to be distributed over the members of this group without respect for the position of individuals on the scale, then it is clear that for any given wilderness preservation project the individual share of the costs will outweigh the individual share of the benefits for all those to the left of a certain point.

Government financing of such a project serves only the interests of those to the right of this point.

The conservationists are hardly willing to give up their fight simply because the benefits of the projects which they propose are not distributed with exact mathematical equality among the entire population. Even conceding this point, they are able to return to the attack with a number of other reasons for including wilderness preservation among the items receiving government subsidies.

One of the most frequently heard of these is the argument of irreversibility. Suppose, it is said, that you cut down a stand of virgin redwood forest to make lumber, or dam a beautiful canyon to generate electricity. In a few years the housing may have less value than you thought, or atomic power may make the dam obsolete, but no matter how much you regret your decision the trees or canyon are gone forever. But if you mistakenly reserve an area for a park and if, in a few years, you find that interest in this particular park is less than you had thought, or if a really pressing need for timber or power develops, you can easily reverse your decision. Therefore, the argument goes, if there is any doubt in the marginal cases of commercial development versus wilderness preservation, it is best to play safe and decide in favor of the latter.

I think the irreversibility argument contains a grain of truth, but that as an argument for government spending on wilderness preservation its importance has been greatly exaggerated. It is simply not true that the destruction of wilderness areas is irreversible, except in the narrow case where the value of an area lies in its virginity *per se*. Pure virgin wilderness, although important and extremely valuable, is only a part of the total land available for recreational use.

To anyone who has been to Vermont during the October foliage season or visited the Smoky Mountains, an area which is in much better condition today than when it first became a park, certain Western conservationists, with their haughty contempt for second-growth woodland, must seem a bit narrow minded.

Many conservationists are extremely suspicious of the concept of wilderness restoration because the idea has often been misused in support of the erroneous contention that our remaining virgin areas need not be handled with care. But by refusing even to consider restoration where it is possible, I think they are doing themselves a disservice in the long run.

For those areas like the largest virgin redwoods and sequoias, where restoration is impossible, there is some validity to the irreversibility argument. Consider Figure 7.2. This little graph shows the value, for each year in the 20th century, of a certain site in its alternative uses as a park and for commercial exploitation. To read the graph for any year you measure the commercial value down from the top straight line to the wavy line; and to measure its value as a park you read up from the bottom. The dashed line in the middle shows the breakeven point. The figure has a wedge shape because, as population and GNP grow, the value of the site in both alternative uses increases. As you can see, although there are some year-to-year fluctuations, the wavy line stays above the breakeven point most of the time, indicating that the best use of the land is as a park, despite the fact that for a few years during the Second World War its current commercial value momentarily exceeded its recreational value. If this land had been logged over or flooded in those years and lost forever to recreation, would this have been a wise use of resources? Without going into technical details, it is possible that because of lack of foresight or temporary emergency conditions this particular wilderness area might have been destroyed and thus lost forever to its best use.[41]

Stated in this form, the irreversibility argument does not indicate that federal ownership and control of our national parks is a

---

[41] Those readers with a background in business or economics will recognize that the ability of the market to insure the best use of resources in cases like this one depends on the ability of capital markets to smooth out irregular fluctuations in the curve of Figure 7.2 by discounting future values at the prevailing rate of interest. If interest rates always accurately reflected the underlying preferences of individuals concerning present versus future benefits, then the irreversibility argument would lose its validity altogether. But if, as is the case in the real world, capital markets are subject to controls and imperfections, and if the rate of interest reflects not the preferences of the community but merely the momentary and perhaps misguided policies of the Federal Reserve Board, it is possible that irreversible mistakes might be made.

necessity for shielding the legitimate interests of conservationists from irreversible damage caused by wars, abnormally high interest rates, or other temporary crises. To the extent that the argument is valid, it does argue for a maximum of procedural barriers and delays to be placed in the way of transferring certain sites from recreational to commercial use.

Figure 7.2 Best land use over time

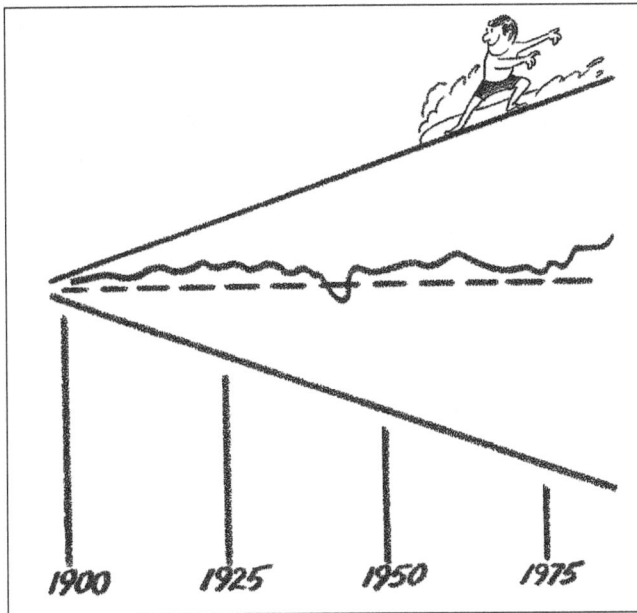

The worst situation would be the one which now prevails for vast tracts of the most valuable federal land where some administrator, at the stroke of a pen, can at any moment make the irreversible decision in question. Conservationists have realized this, and have lobbied for legislation like the Wilderness Bill, which in effect requires that the stroke of the pen be made by Congress, not an administrative agency. This clearly is a help, since as we all know, Congressional decision making is slow and replete with procedural delays. But Congressional decision making is also subject to strong pressures from commercial interests, and in time of war from military interests as well. Wouldn't it be safer if the conservationists themselves had control over these irreversible decisions, rather than relying on the whim of a bureaucrat or the treachery of a politician? If, let us say, the Sierra Club owned the site in question, they would sell it to be logged only if they were pretty sure that the decision was a wise one, only if, for example, the price were high enough to purchase or improve a superior site elsewhere. If conservationists really wanted to lock this site into use as a park, they could not only buy it but write a covenant into the deed which would prevent its sale for commercial use even by future administrators of the Club itself.

In sum, the irreversibility argument turns out to work not in favor of extending our national park system as it now exists but of turning it into a system of private parks to provide surer protection for the future!

As soon as the subject of selling the national parks to the Sierra Club is raised, conservationists come up with another set of arguments in *favor* of government action, which I will call the organizational arguments. Commercial interests, it is said, are concentrated and well-organized, while conservation interests are badly organized and diffuse. Thus, commercial interests would be able to raise the money to outbid the conservationists, even if the latter might actually be able to make better use of the land. This argument can take several forms. Let's see what truth there is in any of them.

It is sometimes alleged that there is a free rider problem with the national parks. This arises not because a few irresponsible recreationists might sneak past the turnstile at the entrance to the park, using it without paying, but because the parks provide benefits, in the form of externalities or spillover effects, to those who *never* visit them. National parks should be considered as a public good, albeit an imperfect one, which like education provides major values to the direct beneficiary, but also furnishes significant external benefits to others in society.

Is this all so? Do you get any external benefits from Yosemite National Park, which you have never visited and which, for purposes of the argument, let's say you never will? If so, just what are these benefits?

For a start we might try to measure the extent of these benefits by the strength of the sense of outrage which you would feel if you read one morning that the park had been converted into a test range for new defoliants for use in Vietnam. That might cause you sufficient pain to mail a check to the Save Yosemite Committee, but you also might not bother, hoping that others would do so and make you a free rider. Perhaps the externality takes the form of the increased range of choice among parks, even though you don't choose to visit Yosemite itself. Or perhaps it is that you can benefit from pictures which Ansel Adams takes there, although you may never see the place with your own eyes. Or perhaps the parks which you do use are less crowded and the entrance fees are lower because Yosemite takes the pressure off.

This is an impressive list. It must be admitted by even the most skeptical that we would be less well off were Yosemite to be despoiled. But does this list of "external effects" justify subsidizing the national park system? If it does, I submit, then subsidy of almost any good or service imaginable would also be so justified, since effects like the above are present almost everywhere in the economy.

Let's look at automobiles, for example. When, a few years ago, a change in federal safety standards took the old Morgan off the market, I felt a definite sense of loss. I would even have sent money to a Save the Morgan fund but for the free rider problem. Do you think that sports car lovers were any less indignant about the Morgan than conservationists would be about Yosemite? Can you prove it? I could claim to be benefited by the fact that the availability of Fords increases my range of choice in cars, even though I have never owned one and probably never will. It certainly is true that production of Fords means the demand for Chevrolets is less than it otherwise would be, hence GM showrooms are less crowded and their prices are lower. I certainly benefit from the production of Ferraris and Maseratis – I don't remember ever seeing one on the street around here, but I have enjoyed looking at some really beautiful photographs. Do all these "external effects" mean that the federal government should subsidize automobile production?

Maybe the external benefits of national parks are quantitatively greater than those that arise from automobile production, organized baseball, or the production of women's clothing. Maybe the external damages of national parks to those who want cheap electricity or cheap lumber, those who enjoy watching movies of lumberjacks and reading stories about miners, and so forth are quantitatively very small. But the burden of quantitative proof lies with the conservationists, and in the absence of such proof no subsidies are justified.

Another form of the organizational argument in favor of national parks is more quickly dealt with. It is sometimes said that conservation groups would be unable to buy the parks because of the sheer organizational difficulty of collecting the money. This objection, I think, is based on the misconception that money would have to be collected door-to-door in advance of purchase, like American Cancer Society contributions. That is not the case. A group which wanted to buy land for a park would be able to borrow the money from a bank, issue stock or float bonds, guaranteeing repayment out of the fees paid by future visitors. What if this stream of future fees were insufficient to pay back the loan? What would be the justification for the park in the first place if only a few would be willing to pay to use it?

I will concede a point to the organizational argument-that at the moment commercial interests do have more ready cash. If all the parks went up for auction tomorrow, the conservationists would be able to bid on very few of them. Consequently, I recommend that the auctioning be done gradually over a period of years, with some of the smaller, less-valuable pieces sold first, to give conservation groups a fair chance to learn the principles of business organization in which commercial interests are already well versed.

Although the public good, irreversibility, and organizational arguments are the conservationists' big guns, there are a number of subsidiary arguments. I will try to deal with these as quickly as possible.

The intergenerational argument states that the wilderness we have now is all we will ever have, so we must pass it on to our children. One generation cannot bind another. We do not have the moral right to deprive our descendants of that which the earth has in limited supply.

This argument would seem to add nothing to the ones already listed. It is in part a variant of the irreversibility doctrine, although that doctrine is even less valid with respect to future generations than to the present. Our sufficiently remote descendants could have, say, all the magnificent groves of four hundred-foot redwoods which we could wish for them, if we just take the trouble to set out the seedlings today. If the wilderness we pass on to our children will be as important to them as to us or even more important (something which certainly seems reasonable, given the high income elasticity of demand for outdoor recreation), then they will flock to the parks in more than sufficient numbers with admission fees which will pay the interest on the bonds floated today to reserve those areas for them tomorrow.

Perhaps the most disingenuous argument of all made in favor of our current system of subsidizing national parks out of tax revenue is that this system benefits the poor, who would be excluded by the high fees necessary to cover full costs. The cogency of this argument is seriously weakened by studies which show low-income families to be strongly underrepresented among users of the parks. Far from benefiting the poor, the subsidy to these parks takes taxes collected from the poor, competes in the federal budgetary process with other programs designed to aid the poor directly, and uses the money to pay for playgrounds primarily for the well-to-do! As a poverty program the national parks are about on a par with the notorious agricultural subsidies.

The people who support this argument are exhibiting about as enlightened a sense of how to help the poor as Marie Antoinette.[42] If you want to help the poor give them spendable cash grants through a negative income tax, or guaranteed annual income, or whatever you want to call it. Then, if these disadvantaged individuals consider that their first priority is to enjoy the great out-of-doors, they will spend their grants on park admission tickets. If, on the other hand, they consider it more important to buy shoes, good food, a decent apartment – or for that matter, beer, cigarettes, or a new color TV – why should anyone else impose other values on them?

A similar argument dispatches the conservationist defense based on the value of wilderness to science. Not that this value isn't real enough, but if science is to be subsidized, the scientists also should be given unrestricted cash grants. They will spend some of this money on leasing special tracts from private park systems, some more on cyclotrons, test tubes, and secretarial help. Earmarked grants to science violate the equimarginal principle just as do earmarked grants to the poor. If your aim is to help science, why dictate to science the way in which the subsidy must be spent?

Last but not least let's deal with the old line about the spiritual and esthetic values of the wilderness on which you allegedly can't put a price tag. True, the wilderness does have spiritual value for a great many people. In the words of John Muir, founder of the Sierra Club and great prophet of the wilderness:

> Climb the mountains and get their good tidings. Nature's peace will flow into you as sunshine flows into trees. The winds will blow their own freshness into you and the storms their energy, while the cares will drop off like autumn leaves.[43]

But who says that spiritual values must be subsidized by the state; and who says they can't be valued in money? This country has, among its great founding principles, the separation of church

---

42 When faced with the starving French masses, the French queen said, "If they have no bread, let them eat cake!"

43 Quoted in *Voices for the Wilderness*, William Schwartz, ed. (New York: Ballantine Books, Inc., 1969), p. 310.

and state, based on the belief that nothing is more destructive of spiritual values than putting them in the pay of politicians. Do our churches languish because they are financially on their own? No! Men and women everywhere, knowing the importance of spiritual values in their lives, translate these values into cash gifts. No compulsory fees are assessed, yet the free rider problem, so bothersome elsewhere, turns out to be a negligible barrier to the financing of religious organizations. Inspirational literature, books on philosophy and ethics, and spiritual music enjoy brisk sales and generate profits for their producers.

Anyone who claims he has spiritual and esthetic values and won't put his money where is mouth is is putting you on. Anyone who puts his hand in someone else's pocket – someone else who may prefer to get his spiritual experience from Bach or Michelangelo or Elijah Muhammad – to finance his spiritual uplift is so short on ethics and morality that I would be willing to subsidize a journey for him to a very remote part of the wilderness indeed!

A Positive Program for Preserving the Wilderness

At the beginning of this chapter I said that I place a very high value on the wilderness experience. This, plus a few simple principles of economics and demography, make me optimistic about the possibilities for preserving the wilderness, provided conservationists develop the will to stand on their own two feet on this issue instead of kneeling in the halls of Congress with their hands out. Here is my four-point program:

1. Absolute top priority goes to the task of getting the government out of the business of *destroying* the wilderness. The government and its administrative alter egos are wilderness enemy number one – the highway departments, which openly refuse to include scenic values in their cost-benefit calculations, but add ridiculously high estimates for equally "intangible" benefits such as the increased comfort of motorists; the Army Corps of Engineers, with their absurd idea of

cost-benefit analysis which counts both costs and benefits as benefits;[44] the Department of Agriculture, which promotes the use of deadly and persistent pesticides and fertilizers to line the pockets of the already oversubsidized farm interests; the AEC, which builds, at the taxpayers' expense, commercially unwarranted "experimental" power stations that release deadly isotopes into the air and pollute our rivers with thermal energy, and which even threatens such horrors as lowering the passes through the Sierras with atom blasts! Then how about the role of government in putting tariffs and quotas on oil, wood products, leather products, meat products, and so forth, thus insuring that the destruction engendered by the production of these items will occur within our own borders rather than abroad? Or how about all the assorted legislators, administrators, and bureaucrats who are in the pocket of offshore drillers, strip miners, sawlog foresters, grazers, prospectors, and dam builders? Next to this incredible list of destructive activities-all of which are financed through the taxes of the same conservationists whose interests they trample upon-the ruination which could be wreaked by private industry unaided pales in comparison. Fortunately, conservation groups are already hard at work on this first-priority assignment.

2. The next part of the plan is of almost equal priority – get the government out of the business of *protecting* the wilderness. As was already emphasized in the discussion of irreversibility, when the last shreds of the most beautiful scenery in the world are at stake, conservationists should want the decision-making powers firmly in their own grip and not in the fickle

---

44 Read the literature on the Alaska Ramparts Dam. It will cost a billion and a quarter dollars. The promoters list this as the first benefit, that is, a billion dollars worth of jobs and payroll for the state. Then they add to this the ouput of electricity as a second benefit! On top of that, they refuse to deduct as a cost the value of the wildlife destroyed, and they make their calculations on the basis of a phony below-market rate of interest [see Paul Brooks, "The Plot to Drown Alaska," *The Atlantic Monthly*, May 1965].

hands of any committee or agency in Washington. Only when the wilderness belongs to the conservationists will it be safe.

3. In order to be ready to take over when objectives 1. and 2. have been accomplished, the third high-priority task is to begin a crash program to convert the wilderness passion which spills forth so freely as a stream of words into an equally abundant stream of dollars. Money talks, and conservationists, unless they are just playacting when they say how much they value their parks, have tremendous potential resources to tap. I am not a specialist in these matters, but I can offer some common-sense suggestions as illustrations of what is possible.

Most important, put an immediate end to queuing as a means of rationing space in recreational facilities which are already overcrowded. When a definite level of capacity can be defined – and this applies to most campsites, for example – charge admission fees high enough to limit applications to available space. This means varying the rate over the course of the season. I can imagine certain key spots where a campground might be filled on Labor Day or the Fourth of July with each camper gladly putting up $100.00. (After all, people already pay prices like this for scalped tickets to the World Series or the Superbowl.) The less wealthy or enthusiastic, and those fortunates who have a more flexible work schedule, will be able to gain admission to the sites for much lower fees on week-days and in off-peak seasons. Waiting in line represents the least efficient, least just, and most easily corrupted form of rationing ever devised. It could be eliminated even while the parks are still government-owned, if conservationists would only have the honesty to tell the park administrators that they are ready to pay their own way and stop trying to take a free ride.

A second useful financial mechanism is the practice of "excess taking," frequently used in New England to finance such establishments as ski slopes. If you want 1,000 acres to build a ski run, you buy that 1,000 acres *and* the adjoining 1,000 acres. As soon as the facility is built, the surrounding land is sold off at several times its purchase price as homesites and commercial properties to those who are attracted to the area by the available recreation. Conservationists have spent much time fulminating against speculators and developers, yet isn't it obvious that wherever a park is built, land values will inevitably go up and speculative profits will be made? So why not get a piece of the action and put these profits to work in a good cause?

The prospects for raising money by both of these methods are greatly enhanced by what might be called Udall's laws after the former Secretary of the Interior who attached great importance to them. Udall's first law: The available open land per capita decreases more than in proportion to the increase in population. (Take 4,000 open acres, 1,000 people, 1,000 residential and commercial acres, 4 open acres per person. Double the population, develop another 1,000 acres for commercial and residential use, and you are left with 2,000 people and 3,000 open acres, 1-1/2 acres per person.) Udall's second law: The demand for outdoor recreation increases faster than in proportion to the increase of GNP per capita.

Take these two laws together and it may be true, for example, that a doubling of the population of an area could increase the demand for outdoor recreation by a factor of nine or ten! Translated into dollars and cents, Udall's laws mean that you are never going to have to worry about demand for your product or how to pay off those wilderness development bonds.

There is also much money to be raised by such methods as conservation window stickers and private philanthropy. By the time the parks go up for auction, the money could be there to buy them, if plans are laid now.

4. The fourth point of the program is to get the conservationists down out of the rarefied air of the high Sierras and develop in them a realistic attitude toward outdoor recreation areas of the non-virgin, non-wilderness variety. As a Secretary of the

Interior once put it, the whole question of recreation is analogous to a flood control project. If you let all the masses of people flow into the parks in an uncontrolled fashion, then a great deal of damage will be done. But if upstream, along the watersheds of the cities and highways, you install control works, diversions, overflow areas, holding reservoirs, and so forth, then the flood can be controlled when it reaches true wilderness areas.

Such a program means buying low-grade, unspectacular, logged-over, or cropped-over areas, especially in the Eastern and Midwestern sections of the country, and restoring them to provide maximum recreational potential. Low-grade wilderness surrogates like these, if properly located and properly developed and managed, can protect the remaining virgin wilderness in two ways, both by the flood control function already mentioned and by producing revenue which can be used to maintain the low-use, high-grade havens of the purists elsewhere.

Commentary

What has changed

When many Americans hear about wilderness or conservation, they think first of the country's National Parks. Remembered visits to Yosemite, Yellowstone, or the Grand Canyon lead them to think of conservation as an intrinsically governmental function. The 1971 version of this chapter challenged this conventional wisdom, and even stood it on its head, by posing the provocative idea of selling off the national parks. Today the national parks remain safely in government hands, but the idea that private property and market mechanisms can play an important role in protecting the wilderness has become much more mainstream.

The Nature Conservancy is probably the best known private conservation organization. It protects some 17 million acres of land in the United States, equal to three times the combined area of the Yellowstone, Yosemite, and Grand Canyon national parks. Another 117 million acres are under its protection around the world. With an annual budget of half a billion dollars, it is the largest environmental charity and eleventh overall on Forbes' list of the 200 largest U.S. charities. The Sierra Club, the National Audubon Society, the World Wildlife Federation, and the Natural Resources Defense Council are other examples of large conservation organizations. In addition to these heavyweights, thousands of smaller organizations promote conservation on a local level through their ownership or management of environmentally sensitive properties. Individual landowners play their part, too, ranging from suburban homeowners who cultivate bird habitat to Ted Turner, at one time America's largest private landowner, who maintains the country's largest private bison herd.

Outright ownership of land, often in forms equivalent to privately owned parks with open access for public, is just one way that conservation organizations use market mechanisms to protect the wilderness. Other techniques include the following:

- *Conservation easements* are agreements by property owners to manage land in a way that provides specific environmental benefits. For example, Ducks Unlimited uses conservation easements as its tool of choice for much of the more than 12 million acres of wetlands that it protects in Canada, the United States, and Mexico. DU negotiates terms of the agreements and monitors them annually to make sure the terms are being met. Conservation agreements are binding in perpetuity, even if the property is sold to a new owner.

- *Mitigation banks* provide a way to avoid a net loss of environmental benefits when development of a property unavoidably causes local degradation. For example, a developer who constructs an access road that damages wetlands in one location can purchase credits that ensure that an equal acreage of wetlands will be restored elsewhere, leading to no net loss. Federal law encourages the use of mitigation banks, but the banks themselves are privately owned and operated. In a typical case, the Mile High Wetland Bank owns 600 acres 25 miles from downtown Denver. In partnership with developers who purchase mitigation credits, it is in the process of restoring more than 170 acres of pastureland to wetland and enhancing the quality of existing wetlands on another 220 acres.

- *Promotion of innovation and investment* is another way in which environmental organizations work with the business community to encourage projects that are both profitable and environmentally beneficial. For example, the Center for Market Innovation of the Natural Resources Defense Council aims to "help implement value propositions that put money into people's pockets while benefiting the environment," and "engage markets in order to design, develop, and implement policies that direct investment toward clean, sustainable technologies." Among its activities are the promotion of clean energy technologies and financing energy efficiency retrofits for homeowners and small businesses.

In short, the private sector has become a major player in protecting the wilderness. Not only has the acreage protected by private initiatives grown, but the range of techniques has expanded far beyond simple ownership. The organizations involved range across the social and political spectrum, from radical activists to conservative, business-oriented groups; from organizations that specialize in lobbying and legal action to those that are completely apolitical; and from purely secular organizations to the Christian environmental stewardship movement, which bases its commitment to conservation on its reading of the Book of Genesis. There is every reason to expect that these kinds of activities will continue to expand in the future.

What has not changed

Although private conservation organizations often work side-by-side with the National Park Service, state park services, and other agencies, conflicts over conservation issues still occur between business and government. Sometimes business is cast in the role of destroyer of the environment, with a government agency standing on the side of conservation, but often the opposite is true. In such cases, it is the job of private organizations to expose, block or mitigate environmentally destructive activities of government.

It is not just by chance that governments often play an environmentally destructive role. As discussed in Chapter 4, one of the chief conclusions of public choice economics is that governments tend to be more responsive to concentrated interests than to those that are widely dispersed. Questions of wilderness protection often pit highly concentrated energy, mining, logging, or fishing industries, whose interests are served by intruding on wild areas, against the more diffuse interests of the pro-conservation public.

Among the most destructive government policies are explicit or implicit subsidies of unsustainable development in wilderness areas. A comprehensive study sponsored by the Earth Council explains the effects of subsidies in these terms:

Prices are the most efficient information system; they largely determine decisions by producers and consumers. When prices do not reflect the full costs and benefits of production and consumption, the true facts about resource scarcity and environmental values aren't made known. Nor are the true costs of producing or consuming goods and services. With nothing better available, people are forced to base their decisions on this erroneous information, causing the overuse of some resources (with a related degradation of the environment) and the underuse of other resources. So there is a direct causal connection between mispricing and unsustainable development.[45]

Subsidies lead to underpricing of the outputs of favored activities, leading to their overexpansion. The Earth Council report lists unsustainable water development, agricultural practices, energy, and road-building as areas in which some of the most destructive subsidies can be found.

In recent years in the United States, energy, mining, and logging activities on public lands in Alaska have been the most high-profile issues, but government sponsorship of environmental destruction is not limited to this country. It is a worldwide phenomenon. Here are just a few examples:

♦ The Canadian government has vigorously encouraged development of large deposits of oil sands that lie beneath the boreal forests of Alberta. Because of the energy-intensive extraction process, oil from those sands contributes much more to greenhouse gas pollution than does oil from conventional wells, and by some calculations, more even than coal. Local environmental destruction is also extensive. One consultant, who is on the whole sympathetic to oil sands development, describes the situation this way: "If a bird flies over a river near the oil sands, the bird dies just

---

45 André de Moore and Peter Calamai, *Subsidizing Unsustainable Development: Undermining the Earth with Public Funds*, Earth Council, online at http://www.cbd.int/doc/case-studies/inc/cs-inc-earthcouncil-unsustainable-en.pdf

from flying over the river. It's that toxic. They are just dumping all the waste into the waterways. If you did that in the U.S. you would be in jail."[46]

♦ Brazil's rainforests have long been a battleground for conservation interests vs. developers. The Brazilian government has sometimes been on one side, sometimes the other. After 2004, rainforest destruction slowed, but in May 2011, the country's Congress passed a reform of the forest code that threatens to greatly accelerate development in the region.[47] Conservationists hoped that President Dima Rousseff would veto at least part of the bill.

♦ In 2008, the mining company Marathon Resources was suspended from operations in Australia's Arkaroola Wilderness Sanctuary for dumping thousands of bags of low-level radioactive waste. Shortly after that, a poll conducted by the South Australia government found that 82% of the pubic were opposed to all mining activities in the sanctuary. Nonetheless, in 2010, the government modified its mining legislation in order to allow Marathon to resume operations.[48]

♦ China's environmental situation is "very grave and is facing many difficulties and challenges," according to the country's own deputy environment minister.[49] Water quality, air pollution, and heavy metal pollution are especially widespread problems. The central government is at least paying lip service to the need for improvement, but local officials,

---

46 Candice Beaumont, manager of L Investments and a member of the Independent Petroleum Association of America, in an interview with Oliver Ludwig published on Seeking Alpha, Nov. 12, 2010, online at http://seekingalpha.com/article/236566-oil-sands-could-delay-peak-oil-candice-beaumont.

47 Reported by ZME Science, May 30, 2011 http://www.zmescience.com/ecology/environmental-issues/brazil-deforestation-rainforest-30052011/.

48 Reported by the Australian Wilderness Society, Dec. 20, 2010, http://www.wilderness.org.au/regions/south-australia/government-gives-green-light-to-more-environmental-destruction-1.

49 Li Ganjie, as reported by Reuters, June 3, 2011. http://www.reuters.com/article/2011/06/03/china-environment-idUSL3E7H30FL20110603

often subservient to the wishes of state-owned heavy industry, fail to implement central directives.

◆ Russia's environmental problems were already grave under the Soviet regime, as discussed in Chapter 1. They are little improved today. In fact, they are so bad that Russian President Dmitry Medvedev considers them a threat to national security that could make parts of the country uninhabitable within 30 years.[50]

In the future, as in the past, striking a balance between conservation and development interests will pose ongoing challenges. In part, the challenges arise from the fact that development interests are often more concentrated, giving them an advantage in the struggle to shape government policy. In part, the challenges reflect the fact that the interest in conservation, although widespread, is not held with equal intensity by all members of the public.[51] In part, the challenges reflect an increasing global population, which, as discussed in the previous chapter, puts greater pressure on the world's remaining wild areas. The best hope for striking the right balance is to maintain vigorous private-sector involvement that makes maximum use of property rights and market mechanisms, working with governments where appropriate, and providing a check on government excesses where needed.

---

50 Quoted by Agence France Press, June 22, 2008 http://afp.google.com/article/ALeqM5gRd76iVIzDU1XjWGgoUw0ShP-xhw .

51 Uneven distribution of public interest in conservation issues can lead to overprotection of some environmental interests while at the same time others are underprotected. As an example, some critics cite the endangered species act, under which "poster child" species such as the spotted owl are protected at great cost, while other less glamorous species are left to go extinct without anyone noticing.

Chapter 8

TOWARD AN ECOLOGICALLY VIABLE ECONOMY

Searching
finance

We began this book by drawing the distinction between the myth of the throughput economy and the reality of spaceship earth. Throughout the intervening chapters we have continually reiterated the theme that as long as our economic system is adapted to the myth and not to the reality of the world we live in, we are in trouble. Even if the human race is lucky enough to escape the worst prophecies of gloom and doom – extinction via nuclear war, massive flooding, a new ice age, or the teretogenic effects of pesticides and herbicides – we are still faced with the inevitable prospect that our throughput economy will simply run out of usable sources and sinks, and that we will have to spend an ever-greater fraction of our Gross National Product cleaning up after ourselves.

So far we have largely confined ourselves to what economists call the microeconomic point of view, that is, to detailed consideration of the ways in which the decision-making context of individual consumers, enterprises, and interest groups could be altered to provide incentives for the avoidance of ecologically destructive activities. Now we will take a brief look at some macroeconomic aspects of the spaceship earth economy which we will sooner or later have to establish, which is to say, we will back off and try to see the problem as a whole.

There was a period during the first years of the last decade when in the economics departments of our great universities the most popular topic in macroeconomics was economic growth. With the inauguration of President John Kennedy it seemed that the Keynesian revolution had been completed and that the problems of economic stability, inflation, and unemployment, which had preoccupied macroeconomics since the thirties, would be banished once and for all. At this juncture the young avant-garde economists turned their attention to the promotion of economic growth as the great panacea which would conquer the next set of problems- poverty, underdevelopment, and catching up with the Russians.

Suddenly the era of growthmanship is over. Today the Young Turks of the economics profession are increasingly questioning the necessity and desirability of economic growth. Many of them would even go as far as the editors of *Ramparts*, who write that "we simply don't need any more Gross National Product, any more unnecessary goods and factories. What we do need is a *redistribution* of existing real wealth, and a *reallocation* of society's resources."[52] The ecologically concerned, it seems, view the abandonment of economic growth as one of those "painful self-sacrifices" that we are called upon to make.

Is there anything of substance to this new wave of antigrowthmanship? Yes, there is. As the reader is already aware, to the extent that the goal of growth meant growth of Type 1 GNP, a grossly misleading measure of human welfare, it was an unworthy goal. And to the extent that each individual microeconomic unit of the economy grew by imposing an increasing fraction of the costs of growth on outsiders, economic expansion meant the growth of inefficiency and waste along with the growth of output. Still, the conclusion sometimes advanced by ecological radicals that we must limit ourselves to a steady state economy eschewing *all* economic growth is, I think, unwarranted. To understand why this is so we must look a bit more closely at the mechanics of our spaceship earth.

Figure 8.1 shows the same spaceship earth model as Figure 1.2, this time with the skin stripped away to allow for greater detail. The basic components of this diagram are again the two boxes labeled "the economy" and "nature." (Let's agree not to split hairs about what goes in which box in certain marginal cases like agriculture, forestry, or fishing.) These two boxes are really much more alike in function than you might guess. Each of them is filled with "capital," a substance which we may think of very broadly as lumps of matter and encoded information capable of allowing work to be performed. The capital in the economy consists of producer capital (machinery, buildings, instruments, and so forth), consumer capital (cars, refrigerators, clothing), accumulated human knowledge (sometimes called "human capital"), and inventories of things like bread and gasoline. Nature also has a capital stock, which consists

---

52 *Ramparts*, May 1970, p. 4. Italics in original.

of such things as the organized body tissues of living plants and animals, the stock of genetically coded information of how to replicate the first component, and certain "natural inventories" like coal deposits and water in high mountain lakes. You could also include such things as the hoards of nuts stashed away by the world's squirrel population.

Figure 8.1 Detailed view of the spaceship earth

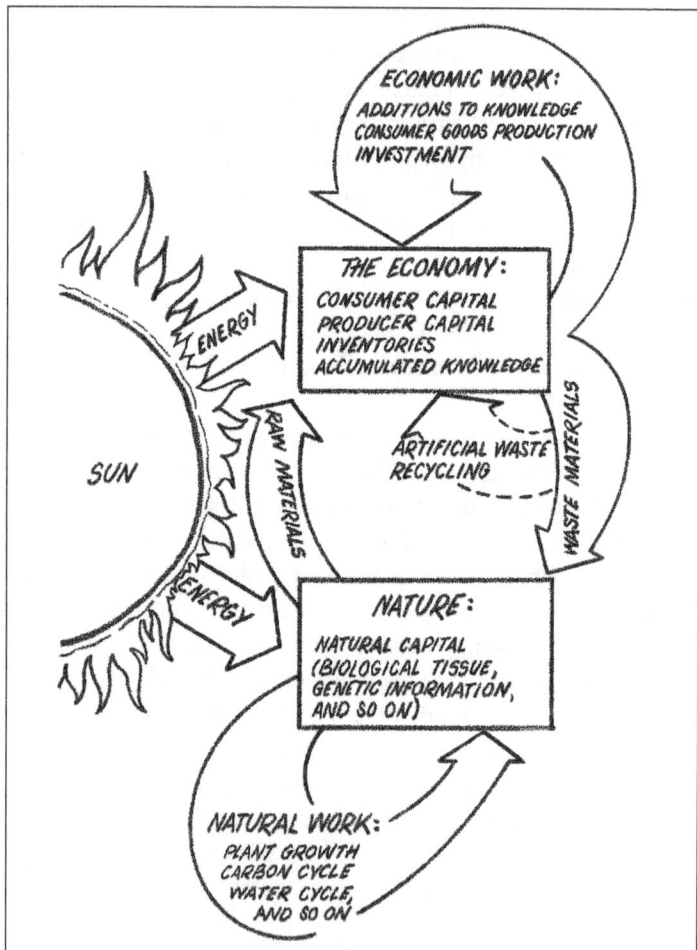

The existence of capital in both the natural and economic realms makes possible the performance of *work*. Economic and biologic subsystems are endowed with the ability to tap certain energy sources and apply the energy to the process of taking up available raw materials and changing their chemical, physical, or locational properties. Whether this takes place on an automobile assembly line or through the process of plant growth, some work is performed while producing useful products, and some waste is generated in the form of products useless to the unit in question.

The concept of *entropy*, if physicists will permit a loose borrowing, is very helpful in understanding the operation of natural and economic systems as working, energy transducing, waste eliminating mechanisms. Entropy, in the broad sense in which we will use the term, means randomness or disorder. The concept of entropy can be easily illustrated with a deck of cards. Build a card house six or seven stories high, and you have a system of low entropy. Knock the house over and you get a random pile of cards on the floor, a system of much higher entropy.

In accordance with the TANSTAAFL principle, it requires an input of energy to reduce the entropy of a system (building the card house). Conversely, a system may release energy in the process of changing over to a state of increased entropy (the card house falling down).

Entropy is of interest to the economist because the goal of all man's economic activity, generally speaking, is to reduce the entropy of his immediate surroundings. (Kenneth Boulding speaks of an "entropy theory of value.") Man builds houses, writes books, weaves clothing, organizes sports events, and so on-all of which represent systems of relatively reduced entropy. Items of reduced entropy are "goods," but in their production certain other items of increased entropy – "bads" – must also be produced. These are waste products. Just as man tries to keep the low entropy goods close to him; he tries to put the high entropy bads as far out of sight as possible.

The only possible case of when man's productive energies are consciously devoted to the increase of entropy is in that peculiar activity called warfare. This may be "the exception which proves the rule," for even in warfare men try to keep the zones of entropy increase as far from their home base as possible.

Now we are equipped to raise the interesting question, what happens to the total entropy within each of our two little boxes, nature and the economy, over time? Let's begin before man came upon the scene. Nature was hard at work for millennia transducing the energy of the sun and creating highly ordered biological systems on the surface of the earth. More and more complex forms of life were evolved and multiplied. Coal beds were laid down. Towering forests sprang up. More and more elaborate libraries of genetic information were painstakingly accumulated.

Enter man. At first, he was part of nature and his appearance counted as a further reduction of the entropy of the natural system. At some point he began to engage in something which we can legitimately call economic activity, and from then on he busied himself for generation after generation with the creation of ever greater and grander low economic entropy zones in the form of artifacts, cities, cultures, and civilizations. Since early man was not able to utilize the rays of the sun directly, he tapped earthly nature for both raw materials and energy sources. Each step in the reduction of economic entropy was made at the expense of an increase in the entropy of nature. This started as soon as men began burning sticks to heat their caves. But for a long time man's economic activities appeared as only the tiniest blip on the fringes of the natural world. Despite the small entropy increase suffered at the hand of man, nature continued to photosynthesize, to evapotranspirate, and to nibble away at the net entropy of the earth's surface.

Eventually the Industrial Revolution came along. Man spread over the whole surface of the globe and multiplied at a fanstastic exponential rate. Enormous tracts of forest were cut down; colossal mountains of iron ore were smelted; vast pools of oil and beds of coal were extracted and their molecules converted into high entropy carbon dioxide with the release of stored energy. At some point, man's ability to reduce economic entropy at nature's expense began to exceed the ability of nature to reduce its own entropy at the sun's expense. (Have you noticed that all of what we have described goes on ultimately at the expense of the sun, which gains entropy every second and will eventually burn down to a cosmic clinker, putting an end, in a few billion more years, to nature and the economy alike?)

That is the phase in which we find ourselves at present. The economy is growing; economic capital is increasing; economic entropy is being reduced; but, in exchange, natural capital is being run down faster than it can be replaced; and natural entropy is rising to the danger point. This can be seen quite clearly in the phenomenon of the rising carbon dioxide content of the atmosphere to which we have already alluded.

It is this destructive aspect of economic growth which worries the antigrowthmen, the ecologists, and the conservationists. Let's stop exploiting nature, they say, and pass what's left of our environment on to our descendents in at least no worse a condition than when we found it. Let's establish a closed-circuit economy which dumps no more high entropy waste products into our environment than can be converted by natural processes back into useful substances. Can this be done and, if so, what are its implications for economic growth?

The answer to this double question depends partly on technology. If we had to limit production of wastes to those of a quantity and quality which could be handled by purely natural cycles, we would have to undergo a very sharp reduction in production of useful output. Fortunately, artificial cycles to supplement the natural ones are possible. Although our current methods of artificially recycling waste products are primitive (even in those cases where we do recycle waste-as in the production of steel from scrap-the recycling process itself often produces waste products of its own) this area of technology is growing very rapidly.

Ecologists and conservationists are extremely suspicious of technology and the purported ability of technology to save the world.

This suspicion is justified by the careless and destructive application of technology by gung-ho engineers and by the glib claims of certain overly complacent souls that technology can repair any damage which technology might inadvertently cause. Yet unless the world is to return to a hunting and gathering society of a few hundred thousand individuals (this is just what certain people with whom I have talked desire) a closed-circuit economy cannot be established without the aid of technology, and in particular that of waste recycling.

But technology alone is not enough. Waste recycling requires organization, and organization requires financing. Who is going to provide the organization and financing of waste recycling, assuming that the necessary technology can be developed? In answer to this question, here are a few passages from Jane Jacobs' excellent book, *The Economy of Cities*:

> One of the oldest forms of waste recycling is the reprocessing of waste paper. One producer of book paper advertises that its papers are more resistant to deterioration from humidity and temperature changes than paper made from new and accompanies these advertisements with striking photographs of New York City, which it calls its "concrete forests." This fancy, that the city is another kind of paper yielding forest, is rather apt; but the metaphor of the waste-yielding mine may be more comprehensive. For in the highly developed economies of the future, it is probable that cities will become huge, rich, and diverse mines of raw materials. These mines will differ from any now to be found because they will become richer the more and longer they are exploited. The law of diminishing returns applies to other mining operations: the richest veins, having been worked out, are gone forever. But in the cities, the same materials will be retrieved over and over again .... The largest, most prosperous cities will be the richest, the most easily worked, and the most inexhaustible mines ....
>
> How will the mines be organized? ... A type of work that does not now exist [will be] necessary: services that collect wastes,

not for shunting into incinerators or gulches, but for distributing to various primary specialists from whom the materials will go to converters or reusers. The comprehensive collecting services, as they develop into big businesses, will use many technical devices. They will install and service equipment for collecting sulfuric acid, soot, fly ash, and other wastes in fuel stacks, including gases that, at present, cannot be trapped. They will supply and handle containers for containerized wastes and will install fixed equipment such as chutes, probably by employing subcontractors. Who will develop the comprehensive collecting services? My guess is that the work, when it does appear, will be added on to janitorial contracting services ....

Comprehensive collectors of wastes may at first derive their incomes like the St. Petersburg trash and garbage processing plant which gets a $3 fee per ton for handling wastes and derives the rest of its income from the sale of its products. Just so, comprehensive waste collectors may at first be paid fees – either directly by those whose wastes they collect, or indirectly by them through taxes, or by a combination of both. This will cover the services of handling wastes not yet convertible or valuable for reuse. But they will also derive income from the wastes they do pass on. As proportions of unused wastes become smaller and the income derived from sales becomes larger, comprehensive collectors will compete for the privilege of doing the collecting work free, just as some collectors of profitable special wastes do now. Eventually they will compete for collection rights by offering fees for waste concessions, again just as some collectors. of special wastes now do. In large cities, the comprehensive collectors will handle and distribute annually many, many millions of tons of materials and will supply immense numbers and varieties of converter industries and recyclers of special wastes.[53]

---

53 Jane Jacobs, *The Economy of Cities* (N.Y.: Random House, Inc., 1969).

What stands between us and Jane Jacobs' future city-mines? A few technological refinements, yes. But technology is not something which just happens; technology is developed largely on demand to service the most profitable and rapidly expanding sectors of industry. Waste recycling would be no exception. What really stands between us and commercially profitable waste recycling is the fact that the government now subsidizes primitive throughput-type waste disposal systems. The subsidy takes the form of city dumps and free or below cost rubbish removal. It also takes the form of public ownership of water resources, into which liquid wastes are dumped without the imposition of user fees. And, in addition, the subsidy takes the form of obsolete provisions in our legal system which allow you to dump your waste into my airspace without threat of a suit from me for the violation of my property rights. If this unfair, inefficient, and ecologically destructive competition were taken away we would already be in phase one of the development of commercial waste recycling (the phase where waste producers pay a fee to have waste removed), even with our present technology. Starting from that point things would soon develop until the flow of artificially recycled waste products back into the economy (shown in Figure 8.1 by the broken arrow) would grow from a trickle into a torrent, which would dwarf the input of raw materials taken from natural sources.

In this way we could eventually settle our entropy balance with the environment. We could adjust the waste-resource cycle so that we passed the environment on to our heirs in just the state we found it or, better yet, we could actually put less than the maximum burden on the regenerative powers of nature and pass it on in an improved form!

Commercial waste recycling will mean increased cost for the producers of many products, and some of these costs will be passed on to consumers as price increases. It will get pretty expensive to maintain such luxuries as aluminum beer cans, no-return bottles, disposable diapers, and jar-inside-a-box-inside-another-box packaging when these gimmicks are no longer implicitly subsidized as they are now. We can imagine that the makers of some of these products will go out of business or, better, diversify into waste recycling or the production of biodegradable wrapping materials.

While the natural world kept on an even keel in this future, or was gradually allowed to regenerate, economic growth would continue inside the box called the economy, fueled by a constant input of solar energy (perhaps fusion energy too – I don't know much about the environmental implications of this) and a constant accumulation of knowledge. Assuming that the population problem is controlled, life within this zone of reduced entropy would become more and more pleasant. Many people would take the fruits of this growth in the form of increased leisure; others in the form of increased consumption of artifacts and services. As long as the latter are all produced out of "clean" Type I GNP, even the old conflict about which of these alternatives is the path to the good life would be laid to rest.

In this ultimate closed-circuit economy of the future a great many sources of social conflict would be absent. With more people paying their own way and fewer living on tax-financed handouts, there would be less reason for the donor to dictate the behavior of the recipient. With lower taxes the level of political tension would be reduced and civil tranquility would be promoted. And with an economy which was not based on the transfer of raw materials from the poor nations to the rich, prospects for establishing peace through the world rule of law would be much improved.

One degree of freedom still remains in our model, an important detail which must be specified before the model is complete. The astute reader (the same one who has been one jump ahead of me all the way through the book), will have guessed what this is. Although we have specified that the economy of the future will eventually adjust to the spaceship like closed-loop reality of relationship to the natural environment, this adjustment could be made at any of a wide range of possible levels.

It has already been suggested that the primitive hunting and gathering economy of our neolithic ancestors satisfied the specification that they took from nature no more for entropy reduction and returned to it no more in waste than could be restored by natural processes. At the other extreme this condition might also be satisfied by a purely artificial economy on a totally sterile globe. Robert Heinlein describes just such an economy in *The Moon is a Harsh Mistress*. The setting is a colony on the moon which, threatened with a cut-off of all imports from earth, has to develop a total economic recycling process for every material used. Nature gives no help at all except in such details as maintaining the carbon cycle with the aid of plants grown under artificial light in synthetic soil with artificially recycled water. All this is written with reference to the moon, but the surface of the earth, according to some of the gloomier (but not to be entirely discounted) predictions, will eventually come close to resembling this state if we don't quit abusing it.

Will we rid ourselves of the throughput myth only at that ultimate point when the nature box of our model has been squeezed absolutely dead and dry? Must we revert to a Neolithic level of existence to avoid this fate? Obviously, the answer is no on both counts. We can stop the deterioration of the environment and settle our entropy balance with nature at any given point whatsoever along the route between these two extremes. The choice is ours.

How shall we choose? Shall we leave it to the Department of Agriculture, the Department of the Interior, or some new-fangled Central Environmental Administration? Shall we take the matter out of the hands of the bureaucrats and turn it over to the legislature, where our elected representatives sit in air-conditioned comfort dividing up the pork? Shall we, perhaps, hold a new constitutional convention on the two hundredth anniversary of 1789, and pass an environmental bill of rights? Or shall we leave the decision up to free men to make for themselves, casting their votes in that most democratic of all forums, the market place?

The reader should have no doubt about which one of these alternatives I am about to recommend. This ultimate macroeconomic decision must be made in the market place, just as all the microeconomic decisions to which we have devoted previous chapters should be. The result would be something like the following.

First, remember that the market can be relied upon to make an efficient decision (one which involves no unnecessary waste or missed opportunities), a just decision (one which involves no violation of the human rights or property rights of any participant), and an equitable decision (one which respects the principle of to each according to his work) only when each man in his every act of production and consumption bears the FULL COST of his actions. How to fine tune the market system to accomplish this end has been the subject of most of this book.

If, tomorrow morning say, everyone in the world started paying his own way, it must be obvious that a great many abuses of the environment would stop. The airlines could never hope to pay off all those suits against the sonic boom, so the SST would be scrapped. Motorists would have to start paying emission charges, and would convert their machines to natural gas or electricity, if they didn't switch to the railroad. Lumbermen would be confined to farming their tree farms. All this would happen very quickly.

It wouldn't take long before commercial recycling firms were set up to mine all those smokestacks, sewers, and garbage heaps. Eventually, as people were made to bear the full costs of having children, and as they learned the full benefits of small families, the population would level off or even gently decline. Within a few years most of the flows in and out of the nature box of Figure 8.1 would taper off to an equilibrium level.

In other areas I think we would and should continue to tap certain types of irreplaceable resources as long as they last. I see no strong reason, for example, for not pumping out pretty much all of the world's deposits of oil and gas. Eventually, exploitation of these resources would cease when the costs of extraction (remember that these would be somewhat increased, since firms would have to take greater precautions about leakages and spillages, and because their depletion allowance tax loophole would be closed) caught up with the price for which the products could be sold. The mining of many metals and minerals would probably also continue for a long time. Under a full cost system things like strip mining of coal would immediately become a losing proposition, but we would probably get pretty much all of the world's supply of lead and tin out of the ground before we were finally reduced to using nothing but reprocessed scrap. The extraction of things like sand and clay might go on almost indefinitely.

All of these continuing extractive activities would help make the world a better place in which to live. While they continued, they would help ease the sharp rise in the cost of living which would occur initially, before Type I GNP caught up with the current level of combined Type I and Type II. And even after they ultimately stopped, the total stock of metals and minerals kept in circulation by the recycling firms would be larger. In no case could these extractive activities continue at a profit where the costs – internal and external, commercial, esthetic and ecological – outweighed these obvious benefits.

While in some respects the natural environment remained much as it is now, and in some was further depleted, in other very important ways the environment would be improved and restored. Foremost among the areas of restoration would be those "great natural sewers" of North America. It might be predicted that within two years after our program began, Wall Street executives would be entertaining their clients at a Hudson River Swimming Club. Even Lake Erie might revive. The air would be cleaner than before, and the cities quieter. If ecology departments in our colleges begin to offer a few courses in business along with science, the areas of wilderness available for recreation should increase.

In short, the world would eventually approach an equilibrium, one in which most of that which we have today would be preserved but with cleaner air and water above and emptier wells and mines below. We can get there, if we get the government out of the business of environmental destruction and let the market teach us that great ecological principle: "There Ain't No Such Thing As A Free Lunch!"

Commentary

Choice and responsibility

Choice and responsibility have been two of the major themes in this book. This chapter rounds out the discussion by returning to the Spaceship Earth model, this time with added detail. The spaceship is now shown to contain two subsystems, an economy and a natural world. Each subsystem, at its core, contains a store of capital. Natural capital consists of living plant and animal biomass, of natural inventories of resources like oil and iron ore, and of accumulated genetic information. Economic capital consists of production equipment, structures, inventories of finished goods, and accumulated education and practical knowhow, or what economists call *human capital*.

Beyond these categories, the list of the kinds of capital needed to make the economy work should be extended to include *social capital*. The concept of social capital is a way of thinking about things that facilitate cooperation and mutual support among members of a community. Often the term refers to relationships like families and social networks, but it can also refer to cultural traits, especially the degree to which cooperation-enhancing values prevail, including trust, integrity, truth-telling, promise-keeping, reciprocity and responsibility.

The economic subsystem can operate in one of two modes in relation to the natural world. When the economic subsystem is operating in its throughput mode, people draw down natural capital by depleting fish stocks, pumping oil, and digging ore out of the ground. They spend part of the resulting production on current consumption and invest the rest to accumulate economic capital. However, the fact that natural capital is finite means that they cannot continue working in the throughput mode forever. Non-renewable resources are used up altogether or become more costly to extract as the best quality sources are depleted. At the same time, throughput production and consumption fills up available natural sinks, making it more costly to dispose of waste products.

In the long run, the question is not one of whether we should operate in throughput mode or the closed-loop Spaceship Earth mode, but rather, at what point we should make the inevitable shift from one to the other. We can do so at any point along a range from an equilibrium in which a human population of a few hundred thousand hunter-gatherers never draw down the original stock of natural capital at all, to the opposite extreme of a completely closed-loop economy with 100 percent recycling of everything.

As the original chapter notes, it should also be possible to find a sustainable equilibrium between the extremes. However, the range of possible equilibrium points looks somewhat different now than it did 40 years ago. In particular, if the predictions of mainstream climate science hold up, it appears that the closest possible equilibrium state that we could strive for would already involve a considerably warmer planet with significantly higher sea levels and new weather patterns. Because of long lags in natural systems, we have very likely missed the opportunity to stabilize the climate where it is now. Discussions of the economics of climate change are already starting to turn from strategies for mitigation to strategies for adaptation.

Exactly what the future equilibrium between the economy and the natural world is like will depend on the choices each of us makes in our multiple roles as consumers, producers, and participants in the process of government. In the language of neoclassical economics, we could say that those choices will be shaped by objectives and constraints, but a simpler way to put it is that our choices will be shaped by values and incentives.

Values do matter. One of the reasons that people have run the economy largely in throughput mode, at least since the rise of early civilizations, is that the pursuit of self-interest, a survival trait bred into our DNA, too easily becomes greed. *Greed* is a term that economists tend to reject as unscientific, but the fact that it is so widely used in everyday speech suggests that we all know what it means. Greed means self-interest that is narrowly focused on material wealth and unrestrained by responsibility, honesty, reciprocity, or promise-keeping. To put it another way, greed means the will to take more than one's fair share of the good and less than one's fair share of the bad.

And just how are we to know what is our "fair share?" The TANSTAAFL principle, which has been the central theme of this book, provides one point of reference. Sometimes we have used the TANSTAAFL principle as a simple statement about reality, a reminder that production of "goods" necessarily entails production of "bads." Sometimes we have used it as a principle of policy design, the idea being that the economy will function more smoothly when people bear the full costs of their actions, including of costs of pollution, depletion of non-renewable resources, and sharing the commons. But we have repeatedly emphasized that the TANSTAAFL principle also has an ethical aspect, one well established in the libertarian tradition. All considerations of efficiency aside, we have a moral obligation to pay for what we take and to make compensation for harms we cause. Taking more than our fair share of the good means taking without paying; taking less than our fair share of the bad means doing harm without making restitution.

A libertarianism grounded in a TANSTAAFL ethic stands in direct contrast to the popular pseudo-libertarianism that marches under the banner of "Don't Tread on Me!" That may have been an appropriate slogan in its original context, when American colonists rebelled against a distant oppressor. Today, though, the slogan is often invoked to mean, "Don't tell me what to do, don't tell me where I can't dig, don't tell me where I can't fish, where I can't dump, or how much I can pollute!" It is the slogan of the productivist, "Drill Baby, Drill" capitalism that the ecosocialists rightly despise.

The bottom line

What next? What is the bottom line? What do we do now?

First, people who want to save the planet need to learn to work across ideological divides. It can be pretty difficult sometimes to get technocratic policy wonks, hyper-ideological Misesians, and Birkenstock-wearing devotees of the Gaia hypothesis to work together, but they need to.[54] Their common interest in the sustainability of life aboard Spaceship Earth ought to make it possible. Conservatives need to stop putting their heads in the sand when they encounter inconvenient truths about the natural world. Progressives need to stop hating capitalism more than they love their planet.

Second, everyone needs to recognize that although values are important, they are not enough. It is all well and good to proselytize, to urge one's neighbors to ride bicycles to work and switch to LED lighting. But that is not enough. Not everyone will listen. Saving the planet will require practical policies with material incentives strong enough to have an impact on the "Drill Baby, Drill!" crowd, the "Don't Tread on Me!" crowd, and above all, on those who are simply indifferent.

Third, getting something done on the policy level will require compromises. Libertarian purists look to property rights, backed by effective tort law, as the ideologically most acceptable way of implementing the TANSTAAFL principle. Deep ecologists see salvation in abandoning an anthropocentric world view, forsaking global trade, and moving to a lifestyle based on indigenous crafts and traditional crops. Whatever the merits of these visions, people who stick with either of them on an all-or-nothing basis are likely to get nothing. I have argued throughout this book that policy will work best if it makes use of the price system and property rights, but in the real world, it may be necessary to accept messy, imperfect versions of those mechanisms, such as gasoline taxes or cap-and-trade schemes.

---

[54] A reviewer scoffed that this will never happen. However, even as I am writing this, I am serving as a member of a citizen committee to provide improved solid waste service for our community, with the combined goals of reducing waste, increasing recycling, and putting an end to wasteful management by the government unit that currently runs the system. Back-to-nature environmentalists, pragmatic MBAs and libertarians dismayed at the way tax money is being squandered all seem to get along just fine on this committee, so long as their activities are focused on a tangible goal.

At the same time, in their search for practical compromises, environmentalists of all persuasions need to be wary of being co-opted into devil's bargains. Too often command-and-control environmental legislation turns out to be little more than greenwash for entrenched special interests. Mandatory stack scrubbers to remove sulfur dioxide from newly constructed electric power plants, part of early U.S. clean air legislation, were an example mentioned earlier in the book. Environmentalists signed on to the stack-scrubber compromise as part of an effort to build a coalition that could get the Clean Air Act through Congress. However, until it was supplanted by a more market-oriented cap-and-trade mechanism, the main effect of the law was to protect existing power plants from the entry of new competitors, and to protect Eastern coal mines and their unions from the competition of low-sulfur Western coal. By themselves, stack scrubbers may even have made the air worse by keeping old plants in service longer.

Fourth, it is necessary to recognize the global nature of today's environmental challenges. In the 1960s, Ronald Coase wrote his seminal paper on the economics of externalities using the example of a railroad that sent hazardous sparks flying into the fields of neighboring farmers.[55] Today's sparks fly farther. Plastic scraps from Spanish greenhouses blow into the sea and harm fisheries off the coast of Turkey. Mercury from Chinese smelters ends up in tomatoes grown in California. Carbon dioxide from gas flared in Russia mixes in the atmosphere with methane from cattle grazing in India to melt the permafrost in Northern Canada.

Persuading the governments of democratic, high-income countries to implement effective environmental policies is certainly a big challenge, but even if it could be done, it would not be enough. Although those countries have accounted for the bulk of global emissions of many pollutants in the past, the situation is rapidly changing. China is already the world's largest emitter of carbon, and India is catching up.

---

[55] "The Problem of Social Cost," *Journal of Law and Economics,* October 1960.

Wealthy countries have limited leverage over poorer countries, many of which are still climbing the upward slope of their environmental Kuznets curves. Aid programs, both private and governmental, may be helpful, at least at the margin, if they are designed with environmental effects in mind. More importantly than direct aid, rich countries should review their own policies to make sure they are not underpricing pollution and resource depletion, in effect offering their own consumers a free lunch while shifting costs elsewhere. Environmentalists in NGOs around the world can coordinate their activities through electronic media, spotlighting what is being done right and what is being done wrong everywhere. These are daunting tasks, especially when governments of developing countries resist environmental reforms, saying to the developed world, "You messed up the planet when you were poor like us, so you have no moral authority to tell us not to do the same."

Readers of early versions of this manuscript have accused me of swinging wildly between the roles of Polyanna and doomsayer. Maybe so. It is easy to see the glass as half full or half empty depending on your mood at the moment. I am encouraged toward optimism where I see things getting better, and I have tried to highlight some areas where that is happening: people who respond to higher fuel prices by changing their driving habits and insulating their homes; not-for-profit organizations that have reestablished vanishing wetlands and flyways; global population trends that pose a variety of challenges to both rich and poor nations, but on the whole do not look nearly as gloomy as many thought 40 years ago.

However, it is equally easy to make a list of things that incline one toward pessimism: a stubbornly short-term bias among policy makers in developed, democratic countries, which often makes action impossible until a crisis arrives, at which point the costs of doing anything are far higher than if they had been dealt with earlier; abysmal governance in many parts of the world that puts the interests of corrupt elites first, the people second, and the environment last.

If reasonable people can be counted on to pick up the ball and work together, the future need not be gloomy. But can they be counted on? They can to the extent that they understand that true self-interest lies in making responsible choices, not in pursuit of a free lunch. They can to the extent that people who understand the TANSTAAFL principle, in all of its scientific, economic, and ethical aspects, get to work and educate those who do not.

Appendix

SCIENCE, PUBLIC POLICY, AND GLOBAL WARMING: RETHINKING THE MARKET-LIBERAL POSITION

Edwin G. Dolan[1]

A survey of market-liberal or libertarian publications and websites finds a large and growing literature on the issue of global warming. Almost without exception, this literature conveys a comforting message: Our planet is in good health. The markets that regulate resource use are working well. The only real dangers come from ill-considered policy initiatives that, if implemented, would do more harm than good. It would seem that the message is well received by its audience — it is repeated, embellished, and applauded with little variation.

In this article, I take a contrarian position, not so much with respect to the science of climate change as with respect to the arguments used by market liberals in support of their message of comfort and complacency. One problem area concerns the proper use of scientific evidence in reaching conclusions regarding public policy. It seems to me that market liberals are often reckless in the degree of certainty they professes regarding climatological hypotheses that are, in fact, still controversial and in early stages of development. A second problem concerns the use of cost-benefit analysis. Market-liberal writers are prone to make

---

1 Reprinted with kind permission from Cato Journal, Vol. 26, No. 3 (Fall 2006). Copyright © Cato Institute. All rights reserved.

Edwin G. Dolan teaches economics at the Stockholm School of Economics, Riga, and the University of Economics, Prague. This article is an outgrowth of a lecture presented at the Liberal Institute in Prague, November 21, 2005. The author thanks the Liberal Institute and Tereza Urbanova, organizer of the lecture, for the opportunity to make the presentation, and those who attended for their many perceptive comments. He also thanks Kitty Dolan and an anonymous referee for additional helpful input.

cost-benefit arguments regarding climate policy that they would never accept in other contexts. Third, the literature on global warming is often weakly rooted, if rooted at all, in the core principles of classical liberalism from which modern market liberalism has evolved. Instead, it is, for the most part, indistinguishable from what is said by conservatives. It might even be said that there is no market-liberal position on this issue—only an echo of arguments made by Republican patriots and the carbon lobby.

In short, the whole issue of global warming policy, as viewed by market liberals, needs to be revisited. This can best be done by going back to some of the classical liberal sources, particularly Friedrich Hayek and John Locke, from which modern market-liberal thought is derived.

Hayek on Liberalism, Conservatism, and Science

A good place to start the rethinking process is with Hayek's essay, "Why I am Not a Conservative" (1960). Hayek identifies a number of traits that distinguish conservatism from market liberalism ("liberalism" without a modifier, in his terminology):

❖ Habitual resistance to change, hence the term "conservative."

❖ Lack of understanding of spontaneous order as a guiding principle of economic life.

❖ Use of state authority to protect established privileges against the forces of economic change.

❖ Claim to superior wisdom based on self-arrogated superior quality in place of rational argument.

❖ A propensity to reject scientific knowledge because of dislike of the consequences that seem to follow from it.

Hayek points out that it is wrong to represent the political spectrum as a line, with leftists at one end, conservatives at the other, and liberals somewhere in the middle. Instead, he represents the political playing field as a triangle with socialists, liberals, and conservatives each occupying their respective corners.

When the political left advances proposals for increased state intervention in free markets, liberals tend to see conservatives as their natural allies. This was especially true in the 1940s and 1950s, the background for Hayek's 1960 essay, when socialism seemed to be on the ascendancy. In Hayek's view, the alliance of liberals with conservatives was reinforced by the fact that, in the America of his time, it was possible to promote individual liberty by defending longestablished institutions, not just because they were long established, but because they corresponded with liberal ideals.

In our own day, alliances between market liberals and modern conservatives are still possible, but as the nature of conservatism has changed, issues have emerged where market liberals' natural allies are found on the political left. Defense of human rights and due process against expanding executive power is one example. Protecting freedom of personal choice against government-imposed standards of morality is another. In these cases the alliance of market liberals with the left is rooted in genuine shared values.

In addition, market liberals and parties of the left may sometimes form a united front to attack the entrenched privileges of state-favored elites. However, in this case the alliance is more opportunistic than principled, since the two allies are likely to see different solutions to the problem of privilege. Whereas the left seeks to overthrow privilege by imposing state regulation, market liberals want to remove regulations in order to expose privileged positions to the influence of competition.

In order to apply Hayek's political triangle to the issue of global warming, we need to address several questions. One issue is what the status is of the privileges and interests of those who are threatened by the possibility of climate change and of those who are threatened by proposed actions to mitigate it. Which of these has the greater claim to the sympathy of market liberals, when viewed in terms of the standards they apply in other areas of public policy? Another issue is what the values are that lie behind the positions taken by various parties to the debate. The issue of values may determine when market liberals can make principled alliances with one of the other corners of the triangle and when they want to make only tactical alliances. Still another issue is what manner of argument should be employed. For example, what is the proper attitude toward the purely scientific element in the global warming controversy? It will be worth taking a closer look at this last issue before proceeding further.

Hayek expresses himself so well on the role of science that it is worth quoting him at length:

> Personally, I find that the most objectionable feature of the conservative attitude is its propensity to reject well-substantiated new knowledge because it dislikes some of the consequences which seem to follow from it—or, to put it bluntly, its obscurantism. I will not deny that scientists as much as others are given to fads and fashions and that we have much reason to be cautious in accepting the conclusions that they draw from their latest theories. But the reasons for our reluctance must themselves be rational and must be kept separate from our regret that the new theories upset our cherished beliefs. . . . By refusing to face the facts, the conservative only weakens his own position. Frequently the conclusions which rationalist presumption draws from new scientific insights do not at all follow from them. But only by actively taking part in the elaboration of the consequences of new discoveries do we learn whether or not they fit into our world picture and, if so, how. Should our mora beliefs really prove to be dependent on factual assumptions shown to be incorrect, it would hardly be moral to defend them by refusing to acknowledge facts [Hayek 1960: 404].

This passage raises obvious questions for the global warming debate. What lies behind the skepticism of market liberals regarding the propositions that the world is getting warmer at a rate that is unusually rapid in climate history, if not altogether unprecedented, and that this apparent trend is likely the joint product of natural cycles and human activity, rather than of the former acting alone? Are liberals correctly rejecting an inadequately grounded scientific fad? Or are they refusing to acknowledge facts for fear that doing so would upset their cherished beliefs?

Perhaps some market liberals believe that global warming poses an unacceptable dilemma that would force them, one way or another, to act against their deeply held principles. They might, on the one hand, believe that the mechanism of market adaptation through spontaneous order is too fragile to cope with the pace of environmental change that some climatologists foresee and, on the other hand, think that the only imaginable policies for coping with climate change involve an intolerable degree of state intervention. If so, they might refuse to consider evidence that a problem exists rather than face a perceived choice between roasting or succumbing to tyranny in order to remain cool.

Fortunately, the supposed dilemma is a false one. Liberals have long acclaimed the market as a way of adapting to change, and climate change should be no exception. For example, Robert Davis (2000) of the University of Virginia has showed how air-conditioning and other market-mediated innovations, have, over recent decades, reduced mortality from urban heat waves.

Also, market liberals should know well that effective environmental policy does not have to take the form of heavy-handed commandand control measures. In dealing with local air pollution, traffic congestion, and land-use issues, market liberals have developed imaginative, workable proposals and in several cases have made headway in getting them adopted. As recently as the 1970s, market-based solutions to environmental problems were regarded as libertarian science fiction. Beginning with the use of averaging, banking, and trading in dealing with lead gasoline additives in the 1980s, and continuing with policies dealing with CFC (chlorofluorocarbon) phaseout, NOx (nitrogen oxide) precursors for acid rain, and continuing with the very recent Environmental Protection Agency measures on mercury pollution, market mechanisms have become very much part of the mainstream. Similarly, congestion pricing for urban roadways, also once regarded as science fiction, is now an established policy in cities like New York, Singapore, Melbourne, and Toronto. The same kind of market-oriented policies should be possible in the case of climate change.

In short, if one takes into account both the market's potential for adapting to change and market-based policy alternatives, there is no reason for market liberals to be anything but open-minded toward ongoing developments in climate science, whether those developments, as they unfold, reveal indications or counter-indications of global warming.

There could, instead, be another explanation for some market liberals' apparent close-mindedness toward the global warming hypothesis. It could be that, when taking a position on issues of climatology, they are speaking not from perceived threats to their beliefs, but out of loyalty to conservative interests with whom they have struck some tactical alliance. For example, policies designed to reduce greenhouse gas emissions, no matter how carefully market-guided in their design, are likely to undermine the interests of politically powerful producers of carbon-based energy. Equally, they are likely to have a disproportionate impact on the United States relative to other, less carbon-intensive, economies. It is understandable that a conservative member of Congress could be pledged to uphold the interests of energy-industry workers or shareholders from his or her home constituency. It is also understandable that a U.S. negotiator at an international conference could work to increase the benefits for the United States of a proposed treaty while shifting the costs to other countries. What is harder to understand is why market liberals would see fit to support such positions, unless for the narrowest of tactical reasons.

Even when fear of change or tactical considerations do not introduce bias in selection and interpretation of scientific material, it may not be wise to base the market-liberal position on global warming too heavily on science alone. The danger is that there is then no fall-back position if future trends in science more strongly establish climate change as a reality. As an example of heavy reliance on scientific material, consider the chapter on global warming from the *Cato Handbook on Policy* (Michaels 2005). Without making any allegation of bias in selection or interpretation of scientific sources, it can be noted that the entire chapter is devoted to purely scientific issues, with the exception of a couple of sentences at the end, which allude briefly to estimated costs and benefits. Some points made in that document also illustrate how fast the scientific ground can shift from under the policy argument. For example, the argument is made that the frequency and intensity of hurricanes in the Atlantic and Caribbean are currently "no different than the regime that was dominant in the 1940s, 1950s, and 1960s" (p. 484). Perhaps this statement seemed safe when it was made in early 2005, but then came along later that year the greatest number of named storms in history, the single strongest storm (measured by barometric pressure), the most economically destructive storm ever, and, to top things off, the latest recorded post-season storm, which lingered on past New Year's Day. Does one bad season constitute proof of a causal link from climate change to storm intensity? As a matter of science, no doubt it does not. But as a matter of argumentation, those who want to urge inaction on global warming might now do best not to mention hurricanes at all.

In focusing too heavily on scientific evidence, market liberals sometimes seem to be making the unspoken concession that, if global warming turns out to be real, then the policy proposals put forward by the nonliberal side are the only ones possible. In that case, if policymakers later do decide to act against climate change, market liberals will have lost their chance to have their voices heard in shaping the specifics of policy design. At a minimum, it would be more prudent to take a two-track approach: "We are not yet convinced that global warming is a reality, but if it turns out to be, here is how it should be handled."

The danger is even greater when market liberals rely on scientific sources that represent a minority within the climatology community. Confronted with the charge that they are relying on minority scientific views, market liberals sometimes reply that science is not a democratic process that establishes the validity of propositions by head-count. They go on to point out that all dominant scientific theories were once minority opinions. This is a weak argument. All mature oak trees were once acorns, but of all the acorns that fall to the forest floor, only a tiny percentage become oaks. Likewise, the chance that any one contrarian in the scientific community will be vindicated is small.

At the risk of digressing from the main theme of this article, it is perhaps worth adding that the perceived validity of one or another hypothesis may not always depend on purely scientific factors alone. In their choice of research fields, and sometimes even in their conclusions, scientists may be influenced by considerations of funding. Funding for science, in turn, depends on the whole range of factors falling under the heading of public choice theory. The interaction of self-interested behavior by allocators of government research grants with the grant-seeking behavior of researchers could plausibly produce systematic biases. For example, research that produces eye-catching findings may be more likely to generate follow-up funding than that which reports ambiguous results. To the extent this is true, public choice considerations may bias reported research results toward the extremes, and in some cases, asymmetrically toward one extreme rather than the other.[2]

A detailed investigation of how public choice considerations operate in the case of global warming would have to deal with several issues. First, it would be necessary to penetrate beyond the widespread feeling among scholars that if only their particular line of research were adequately funded, their point of view would become the generally accepted one. Complaints of this kind, often accompanied by accusations of bias by grantors, can be found in any field of study, whether economics, climatology, or women's studies. What is needed is some way to sort the naïvely self-justifying allegations from the valid ones.

Another issue to be addressed is the relationship between political pressures at various levels of government. In one recently publicized case, James Hansen of NASA reported political pressures to suppress his findings confirming climate change. On the other hand, some observers believe that at the operational level, where specific funding requests are considered, there is a bias in favor of projects that tend to confirm global warming. For example, Margaret Kris (2005) cites Jeff Kueter, president of the George C. Marshall Institute, as arguing that "White House policy is not filtering down to career bureaucrats" when it comes to funding of

---

2   For a discussion of biases in government funding of scientific research, see Savage (1999). Biases in corporate funding of research have been the subject of a series of conferences held by the Center for Science and the Public Interest.

global warming research. It appears likely that there are conflicting biases at different levels of the government bureaucracy.

Finally, a thorough study of the issue of biases in research funding would have to take into account private as well as public sources of funding. Private funding can sometimes be available on a surprisingly generous scale for minority science. For example, Randall Mills and his company Blacklight Power have attracted some $50 million in private funding for research into hydrogen energy that is based on theories that lie far outside the mainstream of contemporary physics.[3] Private funding serves as a healthy factor protecting minority science from establishment bias but, in other cases, it is alleged to be a source of bias itself. For example, organizations opposing genetically modified crops complain that their views are swamped by masses of supposedly biased research funded by agribusinesses. In the field of climate science, there are reports of bias both for and against the global warming hypothesis with regard to funding from private foundations and energy-industry sources (Kris 2005).

Fascinating as these issues are, they are tangential to the theme of this article. For present purposes, it will be enough to treat public choice considerations as an additional source of uncertainty that must be faced by policymakers, who must worry not only about complex scientific arguments, but also about whether the researcers involved are being objective. We will return to the consequences of uncertainty in a later section of this article.

Climate Change and Property Rights: A Lockean Perspective

If the market liberal position on global warming cannot rely on science alone, what should it be built on? The answer, to take the lead of market-liberal thinking as applied to other environmental

---

3   For an account of Mills's work and funding sources, see Matthews (2006).

issues, is a theory of property rights.[4] Following our plan to go back to first principles, we can begin with the writings of John Locke (1690), whose views on property rights and just government are the very cornerstone of classical liberalism.

Locke's thinking on property can be summarized in terms of three rights and three corresponding duties:

Rights:[5]

* ❖ to property in one's own person
* ❖ to property in the fruits of one's own labor
* ❖ to property in land and natural resources taken from nature when mixed with one's own labor

Duties:[6]

* ❖ to abstain from harming others
* ❖ to abstain from taking property of others
* ❖ to leave enough and as good for others when taking from the common

---

4   A seminal source is Ronald Coase (1960). His analysis of pollution and property rights, as well as the importance of transaction costs in understanding the relationship between the two, is now widely accepted by market liberals. The same cannot be said of some of the policy conclusions that Coase, and others since, draw from the analysis in the 1960 article. For a critique of Coase from a property-rights viewpoint, see Cordato (2004).

5   Though the earth, and all inferior creatures, be common to all men, yet every man has a property in his own person: this no body has any right to but himself. The labour of his body, and the work of his hands, we may say, are properly his. Whatsoever then he removes out of the state that nature hath provided, and left it in, he hath mixed his labour with, and joined to it something that is his own, and thereby makes it his property. It being by him removed from the common state nature hath placed it in, it hath by this labour something annexed to it, that excludes the common right of other men: for this labour being the unquestionable property of the labourer, no man but he can have a right to what that is once joined to, at least where there is enough, and as good, left in common for others" (Locke 1690: chap. 5, sec. 27). That the principle for acquiring property applies not just to nuts and berries, but to the land itself, is made clear in Locke (1690: chap. 5, sec. 32): "As much land as a man tills, plants, improves, cultivates, and can use the product of, so much is his property. He by his labour does, as it were, inclose it from the common."

6   With regard to the first two duties, Locke (1690: chap. 2, sec. 6) writes, "The state of nature has a law of nature to govern it, which obliges every one: and reason, which is that law, teaches all mankind, who will but consult it, that being all equal and independent, no one ought to harm another in his life, health, liberty, or possessions." The third duty is given, among other places, in the admonition to leave "enough, and as good, . . . for others" (chap. 5, sec. 27).

The rights and duties are inseparable. One cannot claim the former without binding oneself to uphold the latter. Because the three Lockean duties are central to the issue of global warming, it will be worth taking a moment to examine them in more detail.

The first two duties are incorporated in another body of principles that market liberals endorse, the English common law. Without implying that seeking legal redress is necessarily the best way to deal with large-scale environmental harms under existing laws and court institutions, it is helpful to use analogies with the law to draw attention to ethical and philosophical parallels between environmental harms and other more familiar harms.

In law, the duty not to harm others is covered by the tort of assault, which means threatening or attempting to inflict offensive physical contact, combined with an immediate ability to do so, with the result that the victim is put in a state of apprehension. If the threat is carried out, battery is committed. Following common practice, when no confusion arises, we will use the term assault as shorthand for assault and battery, the combined making and acting on a threat.

The duty not to harm others in their property is covered by the common law tort of trespass. According to one standard legal source, the tort of trespass to land occurs "any time a person, without permission, enters onto land that is owned by another, or causes anything or anyone to enter onto the land or remains on the land, or permits anything to remain on it" (Jentz et al. 1993: 99). Actual harm is not an essential element of this tort. Trespass to personal property occurs "whenever any individual unlawfully harms the personal property of another or otherwise interferes with the personal property owner's right to exclusive possession and enjoyment of that property." Assault and trespass were well established in common law at the time Locke was writing. More recently, both have become codified as part of criminal law.

Certain defenses are allowed against a charge of assault or trespass. Consent of the victim is one. Also, if no causal relationship can be shown between the action of the defendant and the offense to the victim, the tort is not proved. However, certain attempted defenses are not recognized as legally valid:

❖ A showing that others have committed the same offense against the same victim without being held to account, so that the actions of the present defendant are responsible for only a small part of the aggregate harm to the victim.

❖ A showing that the defendant gained benefits from the tort, the value of which exceeds the costs to the victim.

❖ A showing that the defendant has committed the same tort in the past without being held to account.

The relevance of these defenses to the case of global warming will be discussed in the next section.

Locke's third duty, to leave enough and as good for others when taking from the common, can be called the duty not to engross. Engrossment, as Locke uses the term, means unjustly acquiring most or all of something at the expense of other holders of common rights. Locke understands that without a restriction on engrossment, the process of taking from the common could lead to unacceptable results. In one of his clearest statements, he qualifies his principles for taking as follows:

> It will perhaps be objected to this, that if gathering the acorns, or other fruits of the earth, &c. makes a right to them, then any one may ingross as much as he will. To which I answer, Not so. The same law of nature, that does by this means give us property, does also bound that property too. . . . As much as any one can make use of to any advantage of life before it spoils, so much he may by his labour fix a property in: whatever is beyond this, is more than his share, and belongs to others [Locke 1690: chap. 5, sec. 31].

Engrossment of land, as opposed to nuts or game, would occur if a person claimed more land than he or she could "improve, cultivate, or use the product of" (Locke 1690: chap. 5, sec. 32).

The duty not to engross has important implications for the process of enclosing land or other resources from the commons—implications that seem not always to be clearly understood by market liberals who enthusiastically cite Locke as a basis for a theory of property. One implication is obvious: The whole or a disproportionate part of the land cannot be enclosed, or privatized, by the first individual who happens to come along. Think of a Walter Raleigh standing on the Atlantic coast of North America and claiming a swath of property that extends westward all the way to the Pacific. Less obviously, it means that the "mixing of labor" principle can never be used to enclose the entirety of any commons even if each person who comes along takes only that modest amount that he or she can use personally. Instead, at some point a scarcity constraint is reached beyond which enclosing even one more small parcel fails to leave "enough and as good for others." Beyond that point further enclosure may occur but, if so, it must proceed using some different mechanism that requires the consent of all who hold rights in common to the unenclosed remainder.

In this regard, Locke contrasts the situation of a country like the America of his day, where land existed in abundance, with that of England, where the scarcity constraint had already been reached. In the latter case, he writes,

> No one can inclose or appropriate any part, without the consent of all his fellow commoners; because this is left common by compact, i.e. by the law of the land, which is not to be violated. . . . Besides, the remainder, after such enclosure, would not be as good to the rest of the commoners, as the whole was when they could all make use of the whole; whereas in the beginning and first peopling of the great common of the world, it was quite otherwise [Locke 1690: chap. 5, sec. 35].

It is not that Locke thinks the remaining land is better used when held in common than when held privately. Quite the contrary, just a few paragraphs later, he asserts that one acre of enclosed land is as productive as 10 or more acres held in common. Still, if the remaining commons is to be privatized, this must happen by the consent of all the tenants in common. To use modern terminology, they must be bought out, not simply expropriated. If the value of the land really increases through enclosure, a buyout should be feasible. But until the actual consent of the tenants in common is secured, justice trumps efficiency. We must either find efficient rules for managing the land that is still held in common, or we must, for the sake of justice, be resigned to live with the possible inconveniences and inefficiencies of common property.

Applying the Lockean Framework

In this section we consider the implications of the Lockean approach for global warming policy. In doing so, we will, for the moment, set scientific uncertainties to one side. We will take it as a certainty that a harmful amount of global warming is taking place and that this warming is caused by human emissions of greenhouse gasses. In the next section we will consider how our conclusions should be modified to allow for the fact that both the alleged harms from global warming and the causal pathways are not, in fact, understood with certainty.

We can start by looking at cases in which warming has an impact on private property rights that have been clearly established. For the sake of discussion, let us cast in the role of victim a Bangladeshi farmer whose private land is threatened by inundation from a few centimeters further rise in the level of the oceans, and may already be subject to more frequent flooding from the small rise in ocean levels that has already taken place. In the role of defendant, we will cast a coal-fired power plant in the American Midwest. What defenses does the power plant have against a complaint of trespass by the farmer?

One attempted defense might be that the power plant in question contributes only a tiny part of present greenhouse gas emissions. Furthermore, it could be argued that the measured rise in the ocean is the product not just of today's emissions but is, in part, the cumulative result of emissions back to the start of the industrial age, the effects of which have themselves been aggravated by coming on top of a natural warming cycle.

As a matter of justice, this defense would fail. We have already seen that it is no defense against the torts of assault or trespass to argue that others participated in the offense. Suppose I am beaten by a gang of youths, but only one of the gang is apprehended. Would we let him off on the grounds that he caused only part of the harm, or on the grounds that his accomplices got away scot-free? Would we allow the defense to introduce evidence that I had been beaten by other gangs in the past? We certainly would not, and the same principles should apply to our power plant.

A second attempted defense might be that any harm to the farmer was unintentional on the part of the power plant. Its owners may have known nothing about climatology or the low-lying geography of Bangladesh. However, this defense of "sorry—I didn't realize it would hurt" would also fail in a court of law. If the underlying act is intentional— in this case, generating power and releasing greenhouse gasses into the air—intent to accomplish the ultimate harm is irrelevant. In law, one is assumed to intend the consequences of one's actions. For example, a drunk driver cannot plead that he did not intend to run into a pedestrian. The court would hold that the act of drinking was intentional, and that impaired driving is a foreseeable consequence of drinking (Jentz et al. 1993: 92).

A third defense might be to invoke costs and benefits. The power plant might plausibly argue that the cost of mitigating the damage, say by substituting nuclear or solar energy for coal, would exceed the cost of the damage, or the cost of adapting to the damage by building a sea wall or purchasing alternative land on higher ground. If correct, do such calculations constitute a valid defense against environmental assault or trespass?

The question is an important one, since the cost-benefit argument is very often invoked in the case of global warming. Typically, cost-benefit studies find that there would be some benefits from slowing global warming, but often they find that the costs are greater than the benefits. For example, a widely cited analysis of the Kyoto Protocol by Nordhaus and Boyer (1999) estimates discounted costs of implementation at about $800 billion to $1.5 trillion, compared with discounted benefits of about $120 billion.

There are formidable methodological difficulties involved in any cost-benefit study of such a large-scale phenomenon as climate change. One problem that is especially important, given the long periods of time involved in global warming, is the choice of an appropriate discount rate. The present value of costs or benefits realized a century or more in the future will either loom large or become vanishingly small depending on the discount rate one chooses.[7] Another important issue is where to draw the line in counting costs and benefits. Should calculations include only direct, or also indirect costs and benefits? As an example of indirect benefits, University of Virginia climatologist Patrick Michaels (2004) calculates that "fossil-fuel powered societies of the 20th century saw a virtual doubling in life expectancy, largely as a result of the technological and scientific development. Because of the number of people affected, this is equivalent to saving about a billion lives." As another example, *New York Times* columnist Thomas Friedman has emphasized in a series of columns that proper accounting of the costs of fossil fuel consumption should include not just pollution and climate change, but also geopolitical costs arising from the way that high energy consumption enriches hostile regimes elsewhere in the world.

These methodological issues, however, are not germane to this article. What is important for our purposes is only that human activities leading to climate change produce some adverse effects, regardless of how large they are or whether or not they are outweighed by benefits. We will therefore set all questions of cost-benefit measurement to one side by stipulating that the costs of mitigating global warming would exceed the benefits of doing so. How should such a finding affect the market-liberal position on global warming policy?

To begin, we should note that a cost-benefit defense is not valid against intentional torts like assault or trespass. In the case of trespass, the common law does not require any demonstration of harm at all. Unless property owners consent to intrusions, they have (with a few narrow exceptions) an absolute right to exclude them. Even in the case of assault, it is not necessary to prove physical harm. Contact that is merely unwanted or unpleasant can also constitute assault. Nor, in the cases of trespass or assault,

---

[7]   Using a modest discount rate of 2.5 percent means that the present value of $100 in costs or benefits 200 years from now is just 71 cents—equivalent to saying that costs and benefits that far in the future are almost irrelevant for today's decisionmaking. For a discussion of the discount rate and other methodological issues in cost-benefit studies of global warming, see Cline (2004). He finds larger present-value benefits of reducing greenhouse gas emissions than do Nordhaus and Boyer.

are defendants allowed to introduce evidence as to their own gains. If I trespass on your property and cut down a tree that blocks my view, I cannot defend myself on the grounds that the increase in the value of my property is greater than the reduction in the value of yours. Similarly, in our earlier example, the gang member who beat me would not be allowed to plead that the thrill he got from administering the beating was greater than the pain I suffered as a result of it. There is no reason why a tort committed at a distance, via greenhouse gas emissions, should be treated differently from one committed at close range with a blunt instrument. The bottom line is: If you intentionally harm someone, you are liable for that harm, no matter how large the benefit you get from your action.

This does not amount to a blanket rejection of cost-benefit analysis as a tool of decisionmaking. Suppose, for example, that a railroad company is considering construction of a tunnel in place of a track through a mountain pass that is sometimes blocked in winter. The proper approach would be to compare the benefits of the tunnel (fuel savings, scheduling improvements) against the costs of digging it, both properly discounted at an interest rate reflecting the opportunity cost of capital. The same approach would be appropriate for a government considering a tunnel on a public highway. But even if the benefits outweigh the costs, liberal principles would require the builder of the tunnel, whether private or public, not just to calculate the costs but actually to pay them. For example, the tunnel will require some land for the entrance, the approaches, and for dumping waste rock. A favorable cost-benefit calculation would not justify digging the tunnel on land not owned by the builder, or dumping waste on someone else's land without their permission. But that is exactly what is advocated when it is argued that no action should be taken against global warming, because the costs of reducing greenhouse gas emissions exceed the gains (the reduction in harm to victims) of doing so.

A comparison can be made with the liberal attitude toward the state's power of eminent domain. Market liberals have long been wary of this power. Although eminent domain is allowed by the U.S. Constitution, market liberals have traditionally argued that it should be used only in rare circumstances, as a last resort, when problems of strategic bargaining, holdouts, or transaction costs might otherwise bring some essential activity to a standstill. Recent attempts to use eminent domain to condemn land for ordinary commercial projects like shopping centers have been almost universally criticized by market liberals. Yet even eminent domain requires that the owners of the condemned property be compensated. Proposals to inundate low-lying coastal property in order to keep Midwestern electric rates low are not usually accompanied by even the fig leaf of a promise to compensate those who are harmed.

Much the same can be said of the argument that adapting to climate change is less expensive than mitigating it. Yes, a case can be made that adaptation is sometimes more cost-effective than mitigation, and a global strategy should of course take both into account. Convincing data to this effect are provided by Indur Golkany (2005). However, to establish that adaptation is more effective than mitigation is only the beginning of the argument for permitting continued greenhouse gas emissions, not its conclusion. A market-liberal position, based on Lockean property rights concepts, would insist not just on a demonstration that adaptation is theoretically superior, but on the actual undertaking of adaptation measures, at the expense of the interests that stand to benefit from continued emissions. Not just that, the true liberal position would insist that actual consent of the harmed parties be secured, rather than allowing the adaptation versus mitigation decision be made elsewhere and imposed on the victims.

Up to this point, the analysis has been artificially simplified by casting the global warming scenario as a clash of clear-cut private property interests, the Midwestern power plant versus the Bangladeshi farmer. This approach has made the problem into something like the example used by Coase (1960) of the farmer versus the railroad, expanded to a global scale. A more complete discussion needs to take into account the role of unenclosed commons as well as private property.

In the case of global warming, the relevant unenclosed commons include the world air-shed, which, in one of its several competing uses, serves as a sink for greenhouse gasses, and the oceans, which serve as a sink for heat generated by the greenhouse effect and a catchment basin for melting ice. (We are still stipulating scientific certainty of these effects.) Whatever adverse impact the Midwestern power plant has on the Bangladeshi farmer are transmitted through the effects of greenhouse gas emissions on these common-property resources. What does a Lockean approach tell us about rights to make use of the global atmospheric and oceanic commons, and about how those rights might be established?

One result of adding common property to the mix is to give our hypothetical power plant a possible new line of defense, namely, the first-use principle. As a simple example of this principle, suppose I build a drag strip in a rural area and operate it for several years without drawing objections from the neighboring farmers. Later, someone buys part of an adjacent wheat field and builds a housing development. According to the first-use principle, the buyers of the houses have no right to complain about the noise of the drag strip. I was there first, and the noise was priced in when the sale of the houses was negotiated. The situation would be different if I built my drag strip in the middle of an established residential area. Then, the first-use principle would cut in the favor of homeowners, and I would either have to pay compensation, shut down, or limit my races to silent electric cars. Reduced to simple terms, the first-use principle is nothing more than the Lockean doctrine that the acorns in the forest belong to the first person to pick them up.

In the global warming case, our Midwestern power plant could argue that it has established ownership rights to the sink-value of the air-shed by emitting greenhouse gasses into it for many years without anyone's objection. No one has the right to come along now and change the rules of the game. If the emissions are to be stopped, it is the power plant that must be compensated for any abatement costs.

The problem is that the first-use principle ceases to be decisive when it runs up against a scarcity constraint, that is, against the Lockean duty not to engross. In the case of greenhouse gasses, it can be argued that energy users have the right to "enclose" air-shed rights under the first-use principle only so long as enough and as good is left for others. Suppose we reach a point beyond which further appropriation of air-shed rights encroaches on the interests of others who have common-property rights to the world's atmosphere and oceans. From that point on, following Lockean principles, further enclosure cannot proceed by unilateral taking. Instead, if emissions are to be increased at all (or even to continue, if the limit has already been crossed), they can only do so with the consent of all of the tenants in common, including our Bangladeshi farmer and anyone else similarly harmed. If the polluters want to gain that consent, they should bargain for it by offering buyouts, side-payments, or financing of adaptation costs.

To be more specific, we could turn from the general issue of climate change to the debate over the Kyoto Protocol. With regard to this agreement, it is often objected that the United States would bear a disproportionate share of compliance costs since its emissions of greenhouse gasses are, at present, farther above the 1990 reference level than those of other industrial nations. Viewed in Lockean terms, this amounts to arguing that the United States should be let off the hook exactly because it has, in the past, been the most extreme engrosser of the world's common property.[8] This is a profoundly illiberal position to take. Defending the rights of property that has been unjustly acquired

---

8   To avoid misunderstanding, the "engrossment" of air-shed rights with which greenhouse gas emitters are here charged is something different from the more general allegation that rich nations use more than their fair share of the world's resources. It is a cliché in certain circles to decry the fact that the United States, with x percentage of the world's population, uses some much larger percentage y of its copper, natural gas, olive oil, or whatever. A market liberal would reply that as long as the greater consumption of high-income countries reflects the fact that they produce more, and as long as they acquire goods through voluntary exchange, not through unilateral expropriation, the fact of producing and consuming large quantities of goods and services does not in itself constitute engrossment in the Lockean sense.

is a conservative position, not a liberal one. It reminds one of arguments made in defense of property in slaves, at the dawn of the American republic, by writers who, in other respects, were staunch disciples of Locke.

The Significance of Scientific Uncertainty

In the previous section, for the sake of discussion, we treated it as a scientific certainty that harmful global warming is taking place and is caused by human activities. In this section, we relax that assumption to allow for scientific uncertainty. The question to be addressed is, can an action that is proscribed when it is certain to do harm become permissible if the harm is less than certain?

To be sure, some people on the market-liberal side of the debate have denied that there is any scientific uncertainty. Statements to the effect that "there is no credible evidence supporting the theory of global warming" continue to appear from time to time (see, for example, Holcberg 2001). Most serious writers on the subject are more cautious, however. They allow that there is some credible evidence on both sides of the scientific debate.

Consider, for example, Britain's recent report on "The Economics of Climate Change" (House of Lords 2005). That report is cited approvingly by many market-liberal and conservative writers as a counterweight to the report of the Intergovernmental Panel on Climate Change (IPCC 2001), a favorite of environmentalists. After hearing from many witnesses, the authors of the House of Lords report agree that "forecasters do seem to indulge periodically in 'end of the world' stories." On balance, though, they conclude, "We do not believe that today's scientists are 'crying wolf': They may turn out to have been wrong in some respects, but the arguments on which they base their case are better researched than in earlier cases" (House of Lords 2005: 20). Even the IPCC report, if it is read closely and not just mined for the most sensational passages, includes a wide range of projections and lists many "key uncertainties" in the literature on climate change.

Furthermore, as mentioned previously, we should also take into account possible nonscientific sources of uncertainty. In addition to limitations of data or theories that are available for interpreting the data, it is possible that reported scientific findings are subject to biases motivated by political, ideological, or grant-seeking considerations. This problem makes it even more difficult to be sure that the whole truth about climate change lies on one side or the other of the debate.

What difference do the uncertainties make? One way to answer that question is to see how we deal with uncertainties in other contexts.

In daily life, we sometimes deal with uncertainty simply by ignoring the worst and hoping for the best. Suppose, for example, a male executive, during a meeting with an attractive female associate, is tempted to take a hands-on approach to management. He knows well enough that any intentional, unwanted touching will constitute the tort of assault. However, he is uncertain, at least in his own mind, whether his touch will be unwanted. To his way of thinking, some women like that kind of thing. If he takes his chances and makes a grab, should he be allowed, if rebuffed, to make the defense that he was not certain that his act would be ill-received? No, he should not. Our executive, and the rest of us too, know that we should avoid intentional acts that have a reasonable probability of causing harm, even if they are not certain to do so. Intentionally taking an action that has a substantial probability of environmental harm is no different.

This does not mean that we must, like members of a certain religious sect, go around wearing masks to avoid inhaling some endangered species of gnat. Sometimes the evidence pointing to possible harm is so tenuous as to approach zero. For example, some people believe that radiation from electric transmission lines causes cancer. However, despite repeated investigation, the scientific evidence supporting the transmission line-cancer link is vanishingly slim. We need not be deterred from building transmission lines. But the evidence of a linkage from greenhouse gasses to global warming is several orders of magnitude stronger, even if it falls short of perfect certainty. It is strong enough to nullify the "I wasn't sure" defense attempted by our chauvinist executive.

At the opposite pole from hoping for the best and ignoring the worst lies the minimax strategy for dealing with uncertainty. This approach focuses on minimizing the chance of a maximum loss. An example from public policy would be the defense system the U.S. government is building to protect against a nuclear missile attack from North Korea. Although the probability of such an attack is small and the efficacy of the defense system is uncertain, a successful strike by even a single nuclear missile would be so catastrophic that it justifies the expense, at least in the opinion of some people who appear otherwise rational. The fact that more lives could be saved, in terms of mathematical expectations, by spending the same hundreds of millions of dollars on, say, diabetes clinics, is, for them, beside the point. To take another example, this time from the private sector, we know that some people, in planning for retirement, invest in a portfolio of stocks, while others buy certificates of deposit or insured annuities. The latter sacrifice the higher expected rate of return of the stock portfolio to protect themselves against the small possibility that a large-scale market crash could have a catastrophic effect on their standard of living.

A minimax strategy is most likely to make sense when the mathematical expectation of loss is hard to calculate and the feared loss is of a nature that would make a qualitative, not just a quantitative, impact on individual welfare. Some of the risks of global warming may fall into this category, for example, the possible disruption of Atlantic currents that keep Europe warm in the winter. The consensus among scientists seems to be that the probability of such an event is small, at least for the near future. However, it could fit the minimax pattern if, as some oceanographers think, the current might, under some future conditions, stop abruptly with a catastrophic impact on the European climate.

When it comes right down to it, the merits of a minimax strategy depend less on science than on subjective risk preference. There is no objective way to prove that a minimax strategy is the best in a given situation, but equally, no reason to exclude this approach from the discussion of public policy. This should be especially true for market liberals, who, in other contexts, are quite comfortable with taking people's subjective risk preferences as they find them. In discussing financial markets, people with greater than average risk aversion are characterized as "prudent," and markets are lauded for their ability to accommodate their preferences. Why is it, then, that when climate policy is being discussed, people with greater than average risk aversion are dismissed as "alarmists" who do not even deserve a seat at the table?

A third approach to decisionmaking with uncertainty, the "reasonable care" standard, lies between a strategy of hoping for the best while ignoring the worst and the strong risk aversion of a minimax strategy. According to the reasonable care standard, when there is risk that some activity may cause harm, one should take all cost-effective precautions. Cost-effective, in this case, means those precautions which, at the margin, have a cost that is less than the resulting reduction in the expected value of harm.

One application of this standard is to the law of negligence. Suppose I own a trucking company, and you are injured when the brakes on one of my trucks fail, causing it to collide with your car. In a suit for negligence, one issue that could arise is whether I took reasonable precautions to avoid brake failure. Did I buy quality parts from a reputable manufacturer? Did my mechanics make regular brake inspections? If it turns out that I tried to save a few dollars by using substandard parts and skipping inspections, I could be judged negligent and required to pay damages. If I did take reasonable care, I would be judged not negligent and the loss falls on you, the victim.

Applied to the issue of global warming, the reasonable care standard suggests that we should take measures to reduce greenhouse gas emissions up to the point where the marginal costs of doing so begin to exceed the expected value of the marginal gains. This is an improvement over the head-in-the-sand idea that we should do nothing at all until we are fully certain about every detail of climate science. Still, applying the reasonable care standard to the case of global warming is open to an important qualification.

In tort law, the reasonable care standard is most widely accepted in reference to negligence, an unintentional tort. However, as discussed in the previous section, emissions of greenhouse gas are better viewed as intentional torts, akin to assault or trespass. When we build a coal-fired power plant, we intend all of the foreseeable results, not just generation of energy but also emissions of carbon dioxide. We just don't know how much damage the emissions will do. Rather than the analogy of brake failure, to which the reasonable care standard applies, the carbon emissions are more like drunken driving. As explained earlier, both the drinking and driving are intentional acts. We are not excused from the consequences of drunken driving just because we don't know exactly what we will hit in our drunken state—a tree, a car, or a school bus. Despite the uncertainty, we are liable for any harm we cause, and we are required to pay damages.

This reasoning does not absolutely mean that the power plant should not be built. It could be correct that the cost savings from using coal rather than solar energy outweigh the expected value of damage done from the incremental global warming, and even true that there is a nonzero possibility of zero damage. Still, that does not excuse owners of the plant from liability for harm. If harm can later be demonstrated, restitution must be made through payment of appropriate damages or investment in adaptation projects.

To put it another way, the presence of uncertainty cannot mend the flaws in the cost-benefit argument that were discussed in the previous section. Remember, the most widely cited cost-benefit studies do not claim that the harm done by global warming is zero, only that the benefit of doing anything about it is exceeded by the costs of mitigation. Earlier we saw that such calculations, when both costs and benefits are known with certainty, does not create a right to take other people's property without payment. By the same token, the reasonable care standard, which is the application of cost-benefit principles under uncertainty, does not offer an escape from contingent liability if intended actions turn out, after the fact, to cause harm that was not certain to occur when the actions were taken. Unfortunately, an acknowledgment of contingent liability is too often missing from market-liberal writings on the subject of global warming. Instead, estimates of the expected value of costs and benefits are treated as dispositive, with the implication that emission sources should be held harmless even if the climatological optimists on whose research the estimates were based turn out to be wrong. This does not, to me, seem a sound position for a market liberal to take. It sounds more like a conservative defense of arbitrary privilege, similar to claims of sovereign immunity made by kings and presidents.

Conclusion

What, then, is the bottom line? What is the proper market-liberal position on global warming? If that position is to be constructed on a sound Lockean respect for the persons and property of others, some of its outlines are clear, even if many details remain to be filled in.

First, market liberals should keep arguments based on comparisons of costs and benefits in proper perspective. The fact that an action produces net benefits, even very large net benefits, does not shield the actor from liability if it also does harm. The relative magnitude of the costs and benefits, or their relative probabilities, is, in this regard, irrelevant. The duty not to harm people in their persons or property is not to be bypassed on the basis of any facile cost-benefit calculus. This is an essential part of what distinguishes the classical liberal tradition from other political theories that would invoke the power of the state to override individual rights in favor of some greater societal utility. This being said, cost-benefit calculations may in some other respects be relevant to the formulation of a market-liberal position on global warming. They may help choose between different mechanisms for implementing climate change policy. They may be relevant to the decision of whether to abstain from possibly harmful actions, or to risk possible harm while accepting a contingent duty of restitution.

And they may be relevant to whether harm is better avoided by mitigation of climate change, or instead compensated through investments that help victims of climate change to adapt.

Second, the market-liberal position should be distinct from a conservative position that defends unjustly acquired privileges. Liberalism in America, in particular, grew up in a Lockean state of nature where it was really true, or at least seemed true, that homesteaders, loggers, grazers, and industrialists could take what they needed while leaving "enough and as good for others." What the environmentalist side of the global warming debate is telling us is that we no longer live in such a world. It is not just that we can take no more from the commons; we have quite possibly already taken so much as to have breached our duty not to engross. To be sure, the science of just how much can safely be taken is not yet perfect. We may be way past the limit already or still a bit short of it. But to cry foul because those who have taken the most are now asked to bear a substantial share of the costs is not liberalism.

Third, market liberals should keep a clear head when it comes to the relationship between science and public policy. It is fine to be legitimately cautious when policies are urged on the basis of weakly established scientific fads. One should be vigilant against attempts to smuggle questionable economic or political assumptions into scientific analysis, as is sometimes done in the global warming debate, and also to possible biases in research produced by grant-seeking and public choice considerations. But at the same time, as Hayek warned, any reluctance to accept new scientific theories must itself be rational and must be kept separate from the regret that the new theories may upset cherished beliefs (let alone that they threaten the financial interests of useful allies). This is a fine line to walk, and I fear that the market-liberal camp may at times have overstepped it.

Fourth, market liberals should think about the implications of their principles not just for public policy, but for their personal conduct. It is fashionable in some conservative circles to ridicule environmentalism as a new religion that calls for a personal morality of abstinence (see, for example, Schlesinger 2005). Perhaps market liberals would not want to describe their beliefs as a religion, but all of the great thinkers to whom they pay homage make it clear that the duty not to harm others in their persons or property is not just an abstract guideline for public policy, but a specific imperative of personal morality. To cede the moral high ground on environmental issues to the left is not just tactically foolish, it is unprincipled. To put it simply, a market liberal should not be ashamed to drive a Prius rather than a Humvee.

These broad outlines of a market-liberal position on global warming leave a great deal of room for debate and discussion. They leave open the whole area of how to design a policy to deal with global warming. Are the flaws of the Kyoto Protocol so serious that it is worse than doing nothing at all? Perhaps so—even its staunchest supporters acknowledge that it has many limitations. Should we act now, based on current scientific knowledge? Or should we wait, while firmly insisting on the principle of contingent liability, being prepared to make restitution should subsequent harm turn out to be greater than optimists think it will be? In formulating global warming policy, should each country act unilaterally, based on a duty to avoid harm regardless of what others do, or is it best to try to negotiate international agreements? If measures are to be taken, what role should be given to market-based mechanisms like tradable permits? How can such market-like devices, if used, be introduced in a way that respects existing property rights? How do such devices relate to Lockean principles regarding enclosure and management of residual unenclosed commons?

By addressing these and other questions, market liberals can make a uniquely valuable contribution to the global warming debate. If, however, they allow themselves to be perceived as ostriches whose only policy in the face of uncertainty is to hope for the best while ignoring the worst, and base their position on climate policy on arguments that they would disdain in any other context, they will end up making no useful contribution at all.

References

Cline, W. R. (2004) "Meeting the Challenge of Global Warming." Copenhagen Consensus Program of the National Environmental Assessment Institute (www.cgdev.org/doc/expert%20pages/cline/ClChan300404.pdf).

Coase, R. (1960) "The Problem of Social Cost." *Journal of Law and Economics* 3: 1–44.

Cordato, R. (2004) "Toward an Austrian Theory of Environmental Economics." *Quarterly Journal of Austrian Economics* 7 (1): 13–16.

Davis, R. E. (2000) "Links between Deaths and Climate Weakening Over Time." *Environmental News* (1 February). Chicago: Heartland Institute.

Golkany, I. (2005) "Living with Global Warming." National Center for Policy Analysis, *Policy Report*, no. 278.

Hayek, F. A. (1960) "Why I Am Not a Conservative." Postscript to *The Constitution of Liberty*. Chicago: University of Chicago Press.

Holcberg, D. (2001) "Global Warming vs. Prosperity." *Capitalism Magazine* (21 March) www.capmag.com/article.asp?ID=418).

House of Lords (2005) "The Economics of Climate Change." Select Committee on Economic Affairs, Second Report of Session 2005–06. London.

Intergovernmental Panel on Climate Change, IPCC (2001) *Climate Change 2001: Synthesis Report* (www.ipcc.ch/pub/un/syreng/spm.pdf).

Jentz, G. A. et al. (1993) *West's Business Law*, 5th ed. St. Paul, Minn.: West Publishing.

Kris, M. (2005) "Lobbying and Law—Cold Cash and Global-Warming Research." *National Journal* (2 April) (www.marshall.org/article.php?id=284).

Locke, J. (1690) *Second Treatise of Government* (www.constitution.org/jl/ 2ndtreat.htm).

Mathews, R. (2006) "The Atom Bombshell that is Splitting Opinion." *Financial Times* (10 March): 7.

Michaels, P. J. (2004) Private communication.

Michaels, P.J (2005) "Global Warming and Climate Change." In *Cato Handbook on Policy*, 6th ed., 479–89. Washington: Cato Institute. (www.cato.org/pubs/handbook/hb109/hb_109–48. pdf.)

Nordhaus, W. D., and Boyer, J. G. (1999) "Requiem for Kyoto" (www. econ.yale.edu/~nordhaus/homepage/Kyoto.pdf).

Savage, J. D. (1999) *Funding Science in America*. Cambridge: Cambridge University Press.

Schlesinger, J. (2005) "The Theology of Global Warming." *Wall Street Journal* (8 August): A10.